CORNISH STUDIES

Second Series

ONE

INSTITUTE OF CORNISH STUDIES

Sardinia Pilchardus
(The Pilchard)

EDITOR'S NOTE

Cornish Studies (second series) exists to reflect current research conducted internationally in the inter-disciplinary field of Cornish Studies. It is edited by Dr Philip Payton, Director of the Institute of Cornish Studies at the University of Exeter, and is published by the University of Exeter Press.

PUBLISHER'S NOTE

The publisher wishes to thank the following for items supplied for the cover design: Brian Edwards, *The Western Morning News*, Ian Murphy, 'Fishes' (Fishmonger, Exeter), Jon Mills, Camborne School of Mines, Robin Wooten, Sharron Robinson, The Trevithick Society, Exeter Postcard Society, Earth Resources Centre (University of Exeter) and the Director of the British Geological Survey (1:50,000 map sheets 351 and 258). The cover was designed by Delphine Jones using a photograph by John Sauders.

CORNISH STUDIES

Second Series

ONE

Edited by

Philip Payton

UNIVERSITY
of
EXETER
PRESS

First published 1993 by
University of Exeter Press
Reed Hall, Streatham Drive
Exeter, Devon EX4 4QR
UK

© Philip Payton 1993

British Library Cataloguing in Publication Data
A catalogue record of this book is
available from the British Library

ISBN 0 85989 413 4
ISSN 1352–271X

Typeset at the Institute of Cornish Studies

Printed and bound in Great Britain
by Short Run Press Ltd, Exeter

Contents

INTRODUCTION

The establishment of this second series of *Cornish Studies* represents an important milestone in the development of the Institute of Cornish Studies (and with it the University of Exeter in Cornwall), and is a significant reflection of the progress made in recent years in the inter-disciplinary field of academic endeavour that is Cornish Studies. Although growing out of the early twentieth-century 'Cornish Revival', and having thus acquired both an 'antiquarian' flavour and a 'Celtic Studies' reputation, Cornish Studies after the War moved swiftly to broaden its base. This broadening, indeed, was reflected in the establishment in 1970 of the Institute of Cornish Studies (part of the University of Exeter, but situated in Cornwall and funded in part by Cornwall County Council), with its first Director - Professor Charles Thomas - insisting in *ICS Bulletin No 1 (June 1972)* that Cornish Studies was nothing less than 'the study of all aspects of man and his handiwork in the regional setting (Cornwall and Scilly), past, present and future'. The incorporation of the emerging Cornish Biological Records Unit within the Institute extended this definition still further to include consideration of the natural and physical environment. As Thomas argued, 'The development of society, industry and the landscape in our fast-changing world is as much of concern . . . as the history of those vast topics in the recent and remote past'. In his inaugural address as Professor of Cornish Studies, Charles Thomas re-emphasised this approach, developing his argument to further suggest that part of the role of Cornish Studies was to analyse (and, if necessary, criticise) those policies and forces that were moulding the socio-economic characteristics of modern Cornwall. In effect, Thomas was arguing for the development of a critical Cornish social science, and indeed by the 1980s Cornwall was beginning to attract the attention of political scientists, economists, environmentalists, geographers, sociologists and anthropologists, as well as contemporary historians, each with their own disciplinary perspective to offer. By the 1990s such an approach had become a significant element of the Institute's activities.

At the same time that Cornish Studies was broadening its academic base and expressing an increasing willingness to address the issues of contemporary Cornwall, so scholars in other disciplines were becoming more aware of the

1

significance of regional and ethnic studies. Hitherto dismissed as parochial and folkloric dilettantism, such studies were now seen as offering important insights into the patterns of territorial diversity (cultural, political, and socio-economic) that had become increasingly evident in Western states since the late 1960s and 1970s. Indeed, the early post-War conventional wisdom that had stressed the apparent 'homogeneity' of modern, Western states was now replaced by a new orthodoxy which recognised the persistence (even resurgence) of diversity. This approach was further reinforced by the events in Eastern Europe and the Soviet Union in the late 1980s and early 1990s, when the collapse of the internal and external Soviet empires drew back the veil of 'Communist homogeneity' to reveal a bewildering pattern of ethnic and territorial diversity. Although in the former Eastern Bloc this process led often to chaos and violence, the lack of means of accommodation making the peaceful resolution of issues extremely difficult, elsewhere in the world (notably Australia) recognition of the creative potential of diversity led to positive policies of 'multi-culturalism'.

Cornwall's place within this diversity is recognised increasingly, and a major role of this publication is to bring consideration of that diversity to a wider public. In this issue of *Cornish Studies* the mix of articles is intentionally catholic, bringing together an international team of contributors to reflect the broad range of our subject from local history to social anthroplogy, but with a particular emphasis on the emerging Cornish social science noted above. A new, tentative (but potentially important) perspective is drawn on the aftermath of the Cornish rebellions of 1497, reminding us that the 500th anniversary of that significant event is already on the horizon. Edwin Jaggard, in an impressive sweep of the contemporary primary sources, sheds new light on the (unequal) contest between Liberals and Conservatives in West Cornwall in the years after the Great Reform Act of 1832, and Margaret James-Korany illustrates for the first time the importance of the 'Blue Books' as sources for Cornish emigration history. Harry Woodhouse, a Caroline L. Kemp Scholar at the Institute, has in the finest tradition of Cornish local history engaged in an exhaustive investigation of church and chapel bands in nineteenth-century Cornwall. Moving to those more contemporary themes, there is an article (prompted initially by a *cri de coeur* from the Cornish Cultural Trust and developed from a paper presented by Bernard Deacon at the Cornish Bureau for European Relations conference on 'Culture, Identity and Regional Development' in March 1991) on the nature of cultural identity in modern Cornwall, while Paul Thornton focusses specifically on the 'tourist gaze'. Caroline Vink offers some preliminary observations on the Cornish ethnoregional movement, while Mary Buck, Malcolm Williams and Lyn Bryant address the intrinsically controversial issue of Cornish housing. Finally, Keith Hyatt presents what must be considered the definitive description of the acarine fauna of the Isles of Scilly.

In all this there is, to a greater or lesser degree, a common strand of Cornish distinctiveness, an emphasis on a Cornish 'difference' which finds its expression in everything from political behaviour to the natural environment. When all is said and done, it is this Cornish 'difference' that is at root the *raison d'être* of Cornish Studies as an area of academic inquiry. It is a 'difference' that exists not in parochial isolation but is an integral part of that wider pattern of European cultural and territorial diversity. This collection of articles, therefore, should be seen as a reflection of that diversity, a window into the life of one small but (we like to believe) unique part of the Atlantic periphery of Britain and Europe.

The efforts of a large number of people have helped launch this second series of *Cornish Studies*, and in addition to the contributors, the University of Exeter Press, and those who kindly undertook to read and comment upon the articles, we should like to thank particularly Adamu Sabo, who with great diligence computer-typeset the material and produced camera-ready copy.

Philip Payton,
Director,
Institute of Cornish Studies,
University of Exeter,
Redruth, Cornwall.

'a ... concealed envy against the English':
A NOTE ON THE AFTERMATH OF THE 1497 REBELLIONS IN CORNWALL
Philip Payton

INTRODUCTION
Recent interpretations of Cornish history have sought to explain culture change in Cornwall in the context of the changing relationship between 'centre' and 'periphery' within the State. Drawing upon the work of Tarrow (and Rokkan and Urwin), a model of dynamic phases of peripherality has been developed, a key element of which is the movement from an 'Older Peripheralism' of cultural and territorial isolation to a 'Second Peripheralism' of social and economic marginality.[1] In Cornwall's case, this movement was seen as the over-riding feature of the Tudor era, with the characteristics of Celtic-Catholic Cornwall increasingly under pressure from the forces of socio-economic, political, and cultural change associated with the centralising policies of the State. Although it is not the purpose of this article to rehearse these arguments once more, it is an opportunity to emphasise that the application of this model to the problem of culture change in Cornwall has - amongst other things - rekindled interest in the nature of Cornish reaction to the centralising tendencies of the Tudor State. With the 500th anniversary of the 1497 rebellions already on the horizon, it is after all timely to look again at those traumatic events in late medieval, early modern Cornwall.

TUDOR CENTRALISM & CORNISH REBELLION
The best modern account of the Cornish rebellions of 1497 is that in Rowse's *Tudor Cornwall*, first published as long ago as 1941 but happily reprinted in 1990, and it and other extant secondary sources are a good starting point for an initial reconsideration of the period.[2] It is evident that Cornish reaction against increasing intervention in its affairs by the 'centre' was already noticeable by 1496, when the tinners - so used to the independence and freedom of action lent by the Stannary system - refused to accept new regulations applied by Prince

Arthur (the Duke of Cornwall) regarding tin-bounding, blowing-houses, and the marking of ingots.[3] Already sceptical, even intolerant of local usages and privileges, Henry VII's response was predictable and swift, suspending the operations of the Stannaries. For the tinners themselves this was a stinging rebuke, while the wider Cornwall was faced with the prospect of a deliberate 'central' challenge to the mechanisms of its constitutional 'accommodation' (of which the Stannary system was an integral and central part, allied closely to the functions of the Duchy of Cornwall and furnishing an aura of territorial semi-independence). This was all the more wounding, given that Cornwall - like Wales - had been generally Lancastrian in its sympathies, the Tudor claims to Celtic-Arthurian legitimacy having perhaps struck a Cornish as well as Welsh chord.

To this not inconsiderable provocation was added in 1497 the burden of increased taxation to finance a war against Scotland. The Cornish argued that they were a special case, and that the defence of the Border was properly the concern of the people who lived there. As the Renaissance observer, Polydore Vergil, explained in his *Anglica Historia*,

> For the men of Cornwall, who live in a part of the island as small in area as it is poor in resources, began to complain that they could not carry the burden of taxation imposed for the Scottish war. First, they accused the king, grumbling at the cruelty and malice of counsellors: then they began to get completely out of hand, threatening the authors of this great oppression with death, and daring to seek them out for punishment.[4]

As Vergil went on to note, so widespread was the sense of injustice in Cornwall, the Cornish rose in open rebellion, the two principal leaders of 'the Cornish fury' Michael Joseph An Gof ('the Smith') from St Keverne and the lawyer Thomas Flamank from Bodmin:

> While the people were thus in a ferment, two men out of the scum of the people, namely Thomas Flammock (sic), a lawyer, and Michael Joseph, a blacksmith, two bold rascals, put themselves at the head of the rising. When they saw that the mob was aroused they kept on shouting that it was a scandalous crime that the king in order to make a small expedition against the Scots, should burden with taxes the wretched men of Cornwall, who either cultivated a barren soil, or with difficulty sought a living by digging tin . . . .[5]

The events of the first rebellion are well known and need not be repeated here, but the rising was amongst the greatest crises of Henry VII's reign, and indeed the Cornish army reached as far as Blackheath on the outskirts of London (overlooking the king's military and political hub in Greenwich Palace) before its eventual defeat. Vergil believed that Henry took pity on the poor Cornishmen, and 'had their lives spared out of consideration of their rustic simplicity'.[6] However, Vergil himself suggested another motive for Henry's compassion (or rather caution), observing:

> Later the king would have ordered that the dismembered corpses of Thomas Flammock and Michael Joseph should be displayed in various places throughout Cornwall, in order that the penalties of treason might be widely known and seen: but when he heard that those who had stayed at home were not cowed by the catastrophe which had befallen their fellows, but were still keen to begin a rebellion if they were roused in any way, Henry changed his mind for fear he might embarrass himself with even greater burdens at a time when he considered it enough to end civil strife . . . .[7]

But despite this wisdom (or at least intuition), Henry's restraint was not enough to prevent a second Cornish rising in 1497, his decision to seek retribution in the form of fines rather than blood no doubt further inflaming (paradoxically) those who already objected to paying the Scottish tax. Certainly, Perkin Warbeck, the pretender, saw his opportunity. Landing at Whitsand Bay and having himself proclaimed 'Richard IV' at Bodmin (Flamank's old town), he gathered around him those yeoman and lesser gentry who formed the heart of Cornwall - Polgreen, Borlase, Retallack, Rosewarne, Trevysall, Antron, Nankivell, Tregennow, Calwodeley, Grigg, Trekenning, Polwhele . . . . Although dismissed by one contemporary observer as 'the most part naked men and rascals, the whole flock',[8] they represented the groundswell of Cornish opinion, men of some stature locally who felt sorely aggrieved. That the Cornish used Warbeck as an excuse rather than a reason for this second rising is evidenced in a description of an incident in Taunton, while the rebel army was camped in Somerset:

> a rebel and rover named James . . . took the provost of Penrhyn (sic), and so brought him unto the forsaid town of Taunton, and there tyrannously dismembered him in the market place, and after shewed unto the people that he was one of the chief procurers and occasioners of the rebellion of the Cornish men by reason that he, being admitted a commissioner in those parts, levied of them much more money than came into the King's use, which caused great murmur and grudge among the commons towards the King, and lastly rebellion as after ensued.[9]

However, this time the rebels got no further than Somerset. Warbeck lost his nerve, deserting his Cornish supporters who then melted back across the

Tamar. Again, Henry VII proved remarkably sparing of blood (only the ringleaders were executed) but the extent of the fines levied against Cornwall meant that 'the Cornish were not only defeated but humiliated'.[10] Fines were exacted on a parish-by-parish basis (Breage 4 marks, St Illogan 5 marks, Grade 40 shillings, St Stephen-in-Brannel 4 marks, Lawhitton 4 marks, and so on), while on occasions individuals were fined - as when Thomas Tregos of St Anthony and Thomas Budockside of Budock paid 10 marks for Master Nicholas Wyse, vicar of Constantine. The lands, goods and chattels of those killed or executed were seized, and enquiries continued in Cornwall with a view to identifying and then attainting the rebels.

REVERSAL OF ATTAINDER & THE CHARTER OF PARDON

Rowse considers that, in the aftermath of 1497, 'exhaustion kept the county quiet for half a century',[11] while Cornwall agrees that 'After 1497 Cornwall retreated into quiescence for another 50 years'.[12] However, it is difficult to gauge the mood of the Cornish in the years after the rebellions. They may, to some extent, have sunk back into their introspective isolation, left relatively undisturbed until the next great intrusion by the 'centre' in 1549. But there is evidence, albeit often circumstantial, to suggest that Cornwall in fact remained resentful and potentially rebellious, a restlessness that required attention and appeasement. Certainly, what one may call anti-English sentiment was observed throughout the subsequent period, with Norden writing in the reign of Elizabeth that the Cornish 'seem . . . yet to retain a kind of concealed envy against the English, whom they yet affect with a desire of revenge for their fathers' sakes, by whom their fathers received the repulse'.[13] Similarly, Richard Carew noted in his *Survey of Cornwall*, published in 1602, that inquiries from visiting Englishmen would often be rebuffed with the retort 'meea navidna cowzasawzneck' (I will not speak English), while:

> One point of their former roughness some of the western people
> do yet retain, and therethrough in some measure verify that
> testimony which Matthew of Westminster giveth of them together
> with the Welsh, their ancient countrymen, namely, how fostering
> a fresh memory of their expulsion long ago by the English, they
> second the same with a bitter repining at their fellowship; and this
> the worst sort express in combining against and working them all
> the shrewd turns which with hope of impunity they can devise.[15]

More specifically, in the immediate aftermath of 1497 Henry VII treated Cornwall with a leniency that was not characteristic of the era or the Tudor regime. Despite the heavy and systematic levying of fines, Henry stopped short of the widespread executions that one might have expected. Indeed, he may have feared that still the Cornish were yet 'not cowed by the catastrophe', and that the strategy for the pacification of Cornwall would needs be subtle and restrained. And, despite the initial intensity of the fines and attainders, by the early 1500s this process was already being reversed. As early as 1500 William Barrett of Tregarne (Flamank's brother-in-law) had been pardoned for his part in the rebellions, and in 1506 there was a spate of reversals of attainder. James Tripcony (son and heir of Walter Tripcony, who was presumably executed after 1497) received the property of his father, and likewise did William Brabyn of St Mabyn (son of the late John Brabyn). Other reversals of attainder in that year included those relating to Thomas Polgrene of Polgrene, Thomas Gosworthdogga of St Crowan, Nicholas Polkinghorne, John Trehannek, and John Tregennow. The property of William Antron of Antron (who had been MP for Helston 1491-92 and was executed after Blackheath) was restored to his son Richard in 1512.[16]

Perhaps more tangible evidence of efforts designed to win (rather than force) the pacification of Cornwall, was Henry VII's Charter of Pardon of 1508. This Charter restored the Cornish Stannaries (but only on the payment of a fine of £1,000; how typical of Henry!) and created new widespread powers affecting both the privileges of the tinners and the legislative capacity of the Stannary Convocation or Parliament. As the writer has noted elsewhere, 'These seem curiously at odds with the general Tudor concern to centralise government and dilute local usages, and, coming so soon after the crisis of 1497, can be seen as renewed attempts to seek the "accommodation" of Cornwall'.[17] The restoration and enhancement of the tinners' rights under the Charter of Pardon of 1508 included the extension of the definition of the term 'tinner' (and thus the jurisdiction of Stannary Law) to include almost anyone connected one way or another with the tin trade, not merely the extractive process itself.

The extension of the Stannary Parliament's legislative power was even more significant. The Charter of 1508 established a Convocation (or Parliament) of 24 Stannators, the Mayors and Councils of Lostwithiel, Truro, Launceston, and Helston (the 'Stannary Towns') nominating six each. More importantly, the Parliament thus constituted was afforded a considerable measure of sovereignty, with the right to allow or disallow 'any statute, act, ordinance, provision, restraint, or proclamation . . . made by the King, his heirs, successors, or the Prince of Wales, Duke of Cornwall, or their Council . . . to the prejudice of any tinner, or any other person having to do with black or white tin'.[18] It was this right of veto that lent the Parliament its ultimate power, and which gave it the Westminster-like characteristics noted by Lewis and the ambience of territorial semi-independence emphasised by Rowe.[19] Extraordinarily, a regime ostensibly committed to increasing centralism and the eradication of local administrative idiosyncracies, and which had already suspended the operation of the Stannary system and defeated two major Cornish rebellions, considered it important to offer Cornwall this new constitutional and territorial compact. The Charter of Pardon of 1508 was, in its way, as significant as the Athelstan settlement of the tenth century or the foundation of the Duchy of Cornwall in 1337. Certainly, it bears comparison with other governmental instruments regarding the relationships between the 'centre' and England, Ireland, Scotland, Wales, and any constituent parts thereof. It reaffirmed and re-emphasised Cornwall's specific place in the constitutional make-up of these islands, so that, for example, in Henry VIII's Coronation procession in 1509 there were:

> the nine children of honour, upon great coursers, apparelled on their bodies in blue velvet, powdered with fleur de lys of gold, and chains of goldsmith's work, every one of their horses trapped with a trapper of the king's title, as of England, and France, Gascony, Guienne, Normandy, Anjou, Cornwall, Wales, Ireland, wrought upon velvets with embroidery and goldsmith's worth (sic).[20]

Indeed, the new King, Henry VIII, announced his intention of restoring the Cornish See, based on either Bodmin or St Germans, and as Rowse has noted, such an action would have done much to reconcile the Cornish to the changes wrought by the Tudor regime. However, the money earmarked for the project was spent on a war with France.[21]

But is there any evidence of a mood of discontent in post-1497 Cornwall, other than the inarticulate prejudice noticed rather later by Norden and Carew, which might explain this apparent need to seek the renewed 'accommodation' of Cornwall and the Cornish? One might point to the church-tower of Uny-Redruth, completed towards the end of the fifteenth century, with its decidedly unflattering gargoyle representations of Henry VII and his wife, Elizabeth of York - an indication, possibly, that the Tudors had fallen from favour in the far west.[22] However, the semblance of an answer may lie in the Cornish miracle play *Beunans Meriasek* (the Life of St Meriasek), written circa 1500 and first performed (presumably) during the era under discussion.

BEUNANS MERIASEK & THE STUDY OF TYRANNY

Although written in the Cornish language and focussed upon the district of Camborne, celebrating a Saint with a cult in Cornwall and Brittany, *Beunans Meriasek* is very much a standard late *vita*, composed in the wider European tradition of miracle drama and asserting the fundamental tenets of medieval Christendom.[23] The play as it has survived is composed of three distinct stories, woven together. Although Robert Morton Nance and others have tended to view this construction as disharmonious, strands of continuity and meaning can be identified. Murdoch, for example, considers that the play dwells upon three grand themes: the relationship between Church and State; the combatting of evil and conversion of unbelievers; and the role of the Saints, clergy, and Virgin Mary as intercessors. The Church-State relationship is expressed in universal terms, with the role of the State shown to be that of defending the Church and avenging its representatives. The victory of the Duke of Cornwall over King Teudar, argues Murdoch, should be seen in this context. Similarly, the overtly Catholic nature of the play, with the emphasis on Marianism, the role of the

Papacy and the obligations of temporal rulers towards it, meant that it had strong political overtones: 'it is not hard to see why the play could no longer be performed a mere generation or so after its composition'.[24] Indeed, Cornwall was to emerge as a focus of popular opposition to the Reformation, the Cornish - in a further demonstration of resistance to the encroachments of Tudor centralism - rising in rebellion in 1549 in defence of both their religion and their language. Cornish priests, particularly, played a major role in the events of 1549, and in the aftermath were singled out for special attention - the vicars of Poundstock, Pillaton, Uny Lelant, and Gulval were certainly executed (as was the Cornish-born vicar of St Thomas, Exeter), whilst amongst those attainted were the priests of St Cleer, St Keverne, St Neot, and St Veep. In that context, *Beunans Meriasek* had become a subversive document, a vehicle for Cornish perspectives as well as a statement of global Papal pretensions.

There is, however, a further view, suggested by Lynnette Olson, which considers that *Beunans Meriasek* was already a subversive document in the immediate aftermath of 1497, reflecting strongly a mood of Cornish discontent. Murdoch has insisted that although the King Teudar of the play may have had historical antecedents, 'any link with the Tudors seems highly unlikely except on an accidental basis'.[25] Olson, however, has argued that the central theme of *Beunans Meriasek* is that of 'tyranny'.[26] This provides the link between the three component parts of the play, and gave it a special resonance in post-1497 Cornwall. Whilst it is possible that the component parts were first written before 1497, and that the choice of Teudar as the tyrant-king was entirely coincidental, the collated version of the play that has suvived from that period is dated 1504 and is apparently an edited performance text. At the very least, the theme of tyranny and the choice of Teudar (Henry VII was known popularly as Henry Tudor) would have struck a Cornish audience as being particularly apposite, while the specific desire to stage the play in 1504 may have been a good indication of the strength of Cornish feeling at that time. As Wooding has commented, Teudar's 'defeat by the Duke of Cornwall may well have been a statement of the locals' disillusionment with the distant king. The fact that the play itself was in the local language, probably not understood by English onlookers, might serve to reinforce the "underworld", or slightly subversive quality of it'.[27]

There is, indeed, an uncanny imagery in *Beunans Meriasek*, conveyed perfectly in Myrna Combellack's excellent English translation of the play, in which the Duke of Cornwall could be construed as fighting not only for the universal Church, but for Cornwall:

> 2205 Of all Cornwall, Duke am I,
> As was also my father.
> A great lord in the country,
> From Land's End to the Tamar.
> I am dwelling in - no lie -
> Castle an Dinas itself,

In Pydar.
And up on the high ground,
I've another castle sound,
Which is named Tintagel,
Where my chief dwelling is found.[28]

The reference to Tintagel is interesting, given its tradition as seat of royal power and it symbolic importance as a source of legitimacy for those who sought to rule in Cornwall.[29]

Similarly, King Teudar's utterances would have sent a chill down any Cornish spine:

2397   I will crush the Duke of Cornwall
       Under my feet, with all his people,
       Just like little grains of sand.[30]

And in similar vein:

759   Well now - Teudar is my name,
      Reigning Lord in Cornwall.
      That Mahound gets holy fame
      Is my charge, without fail,
      Both far and near.
      Whoever worships any
      Other God shall have many
      Pains: and a cruel death, I fear.[31]

Stripped of it religious allusions (Mahound is Mohammed), the above might be seen to have an additional temporal message, and it is interesting that Murdoch agrees that Teudar is 'seen as an interloper in Cornwall',[32] an outsider imposing his power. In the final component of the play, an unnamed Tyrant asserts the nature of his power in terms that would again have struck a chord in post-1497 Cornwall:

3208   I am a Tyrant without
       Equal, prince under the sun.
       Though mad and rough men, no doubt,
       Will fight me . . . .[33]

CONCLUSION

The extent to which the collation (and presumed public performance) in 1504 of an edition of *Beunans Meriasek* did reflect an underlying resentment in Cornwall is certain to attract more extensive academic debate and further research. However, taken together with other glimpses and evidences, and set alongside the important fact of the Charter of Pardon of 1508, it does begin to hint at a Cornwall that was indeed restless and - from the perspective of a 'centre' that had already been challenged seriously by the Cornish - in need of renewed 'accommodation'. There is no doubt that the impact of Tudor centralism - the desire to control local usages, the more uniform imposition of taxation, and (later) the Reformation - wrought profound changes in the nature of Cornwall as a peripheral appendage of the English State, and further re-assessment of that process may not not only tell us more about the Cornish experience but also shed more light upon the wider development of the relationship between 'centre' and 'periphery' in what was to become, eventually, the United Kingdom.

REFERENCES

1. Philip Payton, *The Making of Modern Cornwall: Historical Experience and the Persistence of 'Difference'*, Redruth, 1992. See also Sidney Tarrow, *Between Centre and Periphery: Grassroots Politicians in Italy and France*, New Haven, 1977, and Stein Rokkan and Derek Urwin, *The Politics of Territorial Identity: Studies in European Regionalism*, London, 1982.

2. A.L.Rowse, *Tudor Cornwall: Portrait of a Society*, London, 1941, republished Redruth, 1990. See also Julian Cornwall, *Revolt of the Peasantry 1549*, London, 1977, and J.A.Buckley, *Tudor Tin Bounds: West Penwith*, Redruth, 1987.

3. Robert R. Pennington, *Stannary Law: A History of the Mining Law of Cornwall and Devon*, Newton Abbot, 1973, p. 13.

4. Polydore Vergil, *Anglica Historia*, in David C. Douglas (Gen Ed.) and C.H.Williams (ed.), *English Historical Documents*, London, 1967, p. 134.

5. Vergil, p. 134.

6. Vergil, p. 134.

7. Vergil, pp. 135-136.

8. *The Great Chronicle of London*, in Douglas (Gen.Ed.) and Williams (ed.), 1967, p. 117.

9. Douglas (Gen.Ed) and Williams (ed.), 1967, p. 118.

10. Rowse, 1941 & 1990, p. 136.

11. Rowse, 1941 & 1990, p. 140.

12. Cornwall, 1977, p. 47.

13. John Norden, *Description of Cornwall*, cited in A.L.Rowse, *The Expansion of Elizabethan England*, London, 1955, republished 1973, p. 45.

14. F.E. Halliday, *Richard Carew of Antony: The Survey of Cornwall*, London,1953, p. 127.

15. Halliday (Carew),1953, p. 139.

16. Rowse, 1941 & 1990, p. 138.

17. Payton, 1992, p. 51.

18. Pennington, 1973, p. 20.

19. G.R.Lewis, *The Stannaries: A Study of the Medieval Tin Miners of Cornwall and Devon*, 1908, republished, Truro, 1965, p. 127; John Rowe, *Cornwall in the Age of the Industrial Revolution*, Liverpool, 1953, republished St Austell, 1993, p. 13.

20. Edward Hall, *Chronicle*, in Douglas (Gen.Ed.) and Williams (ed.), 1967, p. 148.

21. Rowse, 1955 & 1973, p. 45.

22. Frank Mitchell, *Redruth Parish Church: St Euny's*, Redruth, 1987, p. 6.

23. Brian Murdoch, *Cornish Literature*, Cambridge, 1993, pp. 99-126. The best and most recent edition (in both Cornish and English) of *Beunans Meriasek* is Myrna Combellack-Harris, 'A Critical Edition of Beunans Meriasek', unpublished PhD thesis, University of Exeter, 1985. A good prose translation is Markham Harris, *The Life of Meriasek*, Washington, 1978, but a superior verse version is Myrna Combellack, *The Camborne Play: A Verse Translation of Beunans Meriasek*, Redruth, 1988.

24. Murdoch, 1993, p. 115.
25. Murdoch, 1993, p. 118.
26. Jonathan Wooding, *St Meriasek and King Tudor in Cornwall*, Sydney, 1992. This pamphlet was produced to accompany a performance of selections from *Beunans Meriasek* (using the verse translation by Myrna Combellack) on the occasion of the First Australian Conference of Celtic Studies in July 1992. The present author is indebted to Lynette Olson for the opportunity to discuss further the theme of 'tyranny' during Dr Olson's visit to Cornwall in 1993.
27. Wooding, 1992, p. 6.
28. Combellack, 1988, pp. 96-98.
29. Charles Thomas, *Celtic Britain*, London, 1986, pp. 64-78.
30. Combellack, 1988, p. 104.
31. Combellack, 1988, p. 45.
32. Murdoch, 1993, p. 114.
33. Combellack, 1988, p. 141

LIBERALS AND CONSERVATIVES IN WEST CORNWALL, 1832-1868

Edwin Jaggard

I

On the first day of January 1835, in the damp chill of a Cornish winter, Edward Boscawen, fourth Viscount and first Earl of Falmouth wrote from his seat at Tregothnan near Truro to Sir Robert Peel, Prime Minister and leader of the Conservative government at Westminster. With a general election looming later in the month Falmouth was deeply concerned to strengthen the Conservative position in the West Cornwall county division, by vigorously promoting the candidacy of his eldest son George Henry, better known as Lord Boscawen Rose. Two Whig-Liberals, Edward Pendarves and Sir Charles Lemon, were the sitting members, Pendarves originally for the undivided county since 1826 while Lemon was first elected in 1831. In the latter year the two Whig-Liberals convincingly thrashed their Tory opponents, and when Cornwall was divided into two divisions in 1832 Lemon and Pendarves were elected unopposed for the West.

The Earl of Falmouth wrote to Peel about the 'urgency of his son's situation'. According to Falmouth, Boscawen Rose faced formidable and unnatural difficulties:

> We had calculated upon much violence and the most determined opposition from the whigs and Radicals, but we could not have conceived that Mr Tremayne should have drawn Sir T Acland and other men of property and influence here, into a league having for its object to stifle at once any conservative attempt upon the plea of wishing to secure the sitting Whig Sir Charles Lemon in his seat.[1]

Like Falmouth, Tremayne and Acland were Conservatives of a kind; however, they were canvassing for Tremayne's Whig-Liberal brother-in-law, Lemon. Even worse, the other influential peer in the division, Francis Basset,

Baron De Dunstanville, who may have countered this unholy alliance was 'unfortunately in a dying state and entirely under the control of his wife Lady, Sir C's sister. . .'.[2] Falmouth hoped Sir Robert Peel could use whatever influence he had with Tremayne and Acland, both former county M.P.s, to prevent their untoward interference. Otherwise, he believed, 'the certain consequence of it must be to extinguish all chance of restoring either part of Cornwall to a sound state of feeling for many years to come - it being out of the question that any one of us can start for either Division when we meet with such conduct from professed Conservatives'.[3] Peel quickly replied that he was powerless to restrain the two Conservative troublemakers, so part of Falmouth's gloomy prophecy eventuated. Apart from one brief interlude in 1841 when Boscawen Rose was successful, between the First and Second Reform Acts West Cornwall became a Whig-Liberal fiefdom.

There have been two explanations offered for this. Forty years ago Professor Norman Gash argued that after the 1832 Reform Act there were a number of counties without a powerful resident aristocracy where the levers of electoral politics 'might reside in the hands of some ten, twenty or thirty country gentlemen of comfortable wealth and independent outlook' who agreed upon the county's representation in Parliament, 'and were not easily amenable to any form of central influence.'[4] Six years after Gash, Brian Elvins in his study of the Cornish reform movement and county politics made a somewhat different point. He acknowledged the influence of what he termed 'the Lemon connection', the web of family relationships within and outside Cornwall, explaining how this demonstrated a strand of continuity in electoral behaviour before and after 1832. However Elvins disagreed with Gash on the question of insularity from central influences, pointing out the deep-seated differences between the two local parties, and the ways in which national issues could exacerbate existing polarities in Cornwall.[5]

In fact the political somnolence of West Cornwall as portrayed in *McCalmont's Parliamentary Poll Book* is quite false.[6] Beneath the generally smooth surface of Liberal hegemony were swirling undercurrents, several redolent of eighteenth century electoral politics, others the direct outcome of 1832. Together they interacted to produce a unique county division between 1832 and 1868: not once in those thirty-six years did the voters have to make a choice between rival candidates.

II

West Cornwall's two members of Parliament were not always those who typically qualified as 'Knights of the Shires' - well established, highly respected members of the county gentry. For example, Pendarves was chiefly a mine owner, with a relatively small estate in terms of acres; by 1826 he was also one of the best known of the Cornish Parliamentary reformers, hence his independence of outlook - a quality thought by many to be essential in a county member - was open to question. Michael Williams too was a mine owner, although his father began life as a mine agent before investing shrewdly and founding one of the wealthiest family dynasties in Cornwall. Similarly Richard Davey exemplified the rapid upward passage (within two generations) of a family of mine agents and managers into landed society.[7]

TABLE 1

WEST CORNWALL 1832 - 1868	
1832 - December Pendarves, E.W.W. ....L Lemon, Sir Charles, Bt .L	1852 - July Pendarves, E.W.W. ....L Lemon, Sir Charles, Bt .L
1835 - January Pendarves, E.W.W. ....L Lemon, Sir Charles, Bt .L	On death of Pendarves, 1853 - April Williams, Michael L
1837 - August Pendarves, E.W.W. ....L Lemon, Sir Charles, Bt .L	1857 - April Williams, Michael ....L Davey, Richard L
1841 - July Pendarves, E.W.W. ....L Boscawen Rose, Lord ...C	On death of Williams, 1858 - July St Aubyn, John L
Lord Boscawen Rose rise to Peerage - Lord Falmouth	1859 - May Davey, Richard ....L St Aubyn, John L
1842 - February Lemon, Sir Charles, Bt .L	1865 - July Davey, Richard ....L St Aubyn, John L
1847 - August Pendarves, E.W.W. ....L Lemon, Sir Charles, Bt .L	1868 - November St Aubyn, John ....L Vivian, A.P. L

The election of Pendarves, Williams and Davey underlined an openly acknowledged fact of life about the representation of West Cornwall. Because the division contained Cornwall's most productive copper and tin mines, the backbone of the local economy, the aristocracy and gentry agreed that the mining interest was entitled to one seat.The other was controlled by the agricultural interest. Sir Charles Lemon, Lord Boscawen Rose and later Sir John St Aubyn were its various representatives, although all had mining interests too. Of the three only St Aubyn was descended from a family whose landed respectability had long entitled them to aspire to a county seat. The Boscawens, with a less illustrious lineage, made several unsuccessful attempts to represent the county in the mid-eighteenth century, thereafter confining themselves to the intrigues of their borough empire.[8] As for Lemon, we shall see his grandfather came from very humble origins and it was new wealth plus his father Sir William's long tenure as a county member (1774 to 1824) which made him an acceptable representative. More importantly almost all of Sir Charles Lemon's relatives were well known Conservatives who actively assisted him when there was the threat of opposition.

McCalmont's list of county members reveals five occasions when seats became vacant: in 1841 when Lemon surprisingly retired, six months later when his successor had to move to the House of Lords following the death of Viscount Falmouth, the occasion of Pendarves death in 1853, Lemon's final retirement at the 1857 general election, and lastly, the death of Michael Williams in 1858. None of the vacancies produced a contested election, yet each sparked great political activity among both parties, sometimes lasting months. Each of the vacancies gave the Conservatives some hope of intriguing their way into a seat, a preferable course of action to the known expense of a contest. Why they attempted this unusual course of action is difficult to understand, but possibly it resulted from several factors: the nature of the Cornish people and their religious beliefs, the state of the voter registers and last but not least, the 'Lemon connection'.

III

Among the most outstanding traits of the Cornish is their obstinately independent outlook on life. In his recent book *The Making of Modern Cornwall* Philip Payton explores the evolution of the Cornish character.[9] Mary Coate, writing on the seventeenth century found 'a definite Cornish personality, conservative, but quickened with a restless and active spirit which drove the Cornishmen to adventure abroad and to litigation and lawlessness at home'.[10] She detected an 'independent spirit', something compounded in later centuries among the middle ranks and lower orders by the unique work systems of tribute and tutwork employed in tin and copper mines, together with the Methodist nurtured creeds of self-help and individual improvement. Together they produced an absence of class-consciousness and even of deference. Independence of manner and outlook were also encouraged by the knowledge that family power, prestige and influence ultimately sprang from some form of wealth. Cornwall's tin and copper mining, and the fortunes to be made in trade, banking, shipping or victualling provided every chance - and incentive - for upward mobility. The Williams family, for example, was an excellent illustration of the wealth which could be amassed in two generations. Under these circumstances there is a strong suspicion that many men, aware of the evolutionary patterns of some of the most prominent families, respected their position and viewpoints, but by no means felt compelled to obey them with a forelock tugging loyalty.

Clearly this was the root of the problem between Reginald Pole Carew (an old fashioned Tory) and Charles Jefferey, one of his tenants, in August 1832. Pole Carew wrote,

As I set some value on your Vote and much more on your good opinions, I am desirous of knowing, what you have seen in my character which makes you suppose that I am capable of recommending you to Vote for a Person for whom your conscience tells you you ought not to vote, or what it is, that you have heard of the Character of that Individual which you can have no Personal Opportunity of knowing, which has impressed you, with the idea, that you could not conscientiously give him your vote.[11]

Lord Valletort was the candidate referred to; Pole Carew believed he was a just, honourable and patriotic man, and what further qualifications were needed for membership of the House of Commons? Despite the brow beating and moralizing Jefferey and his brother remained adamant; they opposed Valletort because he would not agree to the abolition of slavery in British colonies. The Jeffereys retained their independence of mind on agricultural issues too, one of the hallmarks of nineteenth century Cornwall's yeoman and tenant farmers.[12]

Press accounts and private correspondence confirm that after 1832 (as beforehand), it was Cornwall's Conservatives who appear to have relied most heavily on landlord influence in county elections. But in the West where there were no contests, the electoral effectiveness of such influence was only conjecture. Whenever there was talk of a prospective Conservative candidate letters were filled with references to the influence of Lord Falmouth, or Mr Basset, or Sir Richard Vyvyan, or the Rogers family of Penrose near Helston. Then realities superseded wishful thinking. When discussing Cornish politics in the West in 1864 Vyvyan grumbled that 'an independence of character which is almost republican (although there is a universal attachment to the Queen) suggests no attempt to strain the landlords' power'.[13]

Reliance on personal influence was a necessity for West Cornwall's Conservatives because rarely did they organise themselves to challenge the Liberals at the registration courts. The spending of money on registering voters was never popular among the party's wire-pullers. As early as September 1832 John Vivian of Pencalenick complained to Sir Richard Vyvyan how efforts were half-hearted and poorly organised.[14] Little changed later in the decade.

REGISTERED VOTERS[15]

	1832	1835	1837	1839-40	1841
West Cornwall	3353	3612	4928	4911	5040

The sharp increase in voters between 1835 and 1837 reflects the success of newly formed Liberal Reform Associations in busying themselves in the registration courts. Meanwhile their rival Protestant Conservative Associations flared into short-lived life then quickly became defunct, making no inroads on the impressive gains of their opponents. However, in 1838 and 1839, led by Lord Falmouth who was grimly determined to unseat one of the Liberals, they did rally. Thus in the Truro district in 1839 Conservative new claims outnumbered the Liberals 169 to 27 while 39 of their objections were sustained to their opponents' 18. Similarly impressive gains were made in the Gwennap district, and it was estimated that overall the Conservatives had gained more than 500 votes in the division.[16] But it was a short-lived effort.

During the 1840s, 1850s and 60s, without a Falmouth to provide leadership, lassitude prevailed. No one was prepared to co-ordinate the Conservatives in an attempt to neutralise the well-known Liberal advantage. When confronted by the realities of registration politics those eager to see a Conservative succeed threw up their hands and did nothing. This was certainly so in 1864 when William Williams believed his son would be an appropriate candidate; Sir Richard Vyvyan emphasised to him and Lord Churston how the register had been neglected by the party and its potential candidates for years.[17]

What was needed to overturn the status-quo was a Conservative who was clearly identified with either the mining or agricultural interest, acceptable to wealthy supporters, and willing to attend to the registrations at least twelve months prior to a general election. Instead the party relied on last-minute nominations, leaving no time for building support or carrying out thorough canvasses. Under those circumstances the Conservatives could do no more than plan to slip into a vacant seat without a contest. To have hoped otherwise would have been futile.

They were also deterred from contests by the obvious nexus between Methodism and Liberalism in western Cornwall. Wesley's eighteenth century tours had a dramatic effect in an isolated region where the Church of England's grip on the population was generally weak. The poorer elements of the population, miners, farm labourers and fishermen, as well as segments of the middle ranks, soon became adherents. Thus by the time of the 1851 Religious Census Methodists of various types far outnumbered followers of the Church of England.

This can be illustrated in several ways. Peter Hayden has demonstrated that in 1851 in a Cornish population of 356,641 only 12.6% of the inhabitants were present at the most numerously attended Church of England services on Sunday 30 March whereas the corresponding figure for Protestant Dissenters (including Wesleyan Methodists) was 32.5%. With a percentage over two and a half times greater than that of the Anglicans, this 'was easily the highest figure for the South West and was one of the highest in England and Wales' [18] Wesleyan Methodism's popularity was also reflected in the number of places of worship.

TABLE 2

PLACES OF WORSHIP - 1851

(Bracketed figures show total worshippers at most numerously attended service)

Division	Church of England	Wesleyan Methodists	Bible Christians
St Austell	18 (1920)	31 (4568)	27 (2531)
Truro	31 (4634)	59 (10,034)	21 (2484)
Falmouth	10 (2312)	13 (3635)	4 (260)
Helston	21 (2194)	36 (3198)	19 (650)
Redruth	19 (2030)	54 (8964)	7 (1350)
Penzance	22 (4315)	58 (9628)	16 (1039)

Source: P. Hayden, 'Culture, Creed and Conflict . . .' and *British Parliamentary Papers, 1851 Census Great Britain: Report and Tables On Religious Worship, England and Wales, 1852-53,* LXXXIX.

West Cornwall's Conservatives could do little to counteract the Liberal-Dissenter nexus. Church disestablishment was anathema to them and the thorny question of abolition of Church rates was another on which their inertia was guaranteed. By the 1860s Conservatives were acknowledging their obvious disadvantage. Meanwhile the Liberals left no stone unturned in consolidating their Wesleyan alliance. This explains why in June 1868 Pendarves Vivian was eager to inform John St Aubyn that 'the Wesleyans have supported me throughout and indeed all the Methodists and we have experienced no opposition anywhere',[19] Three weeks later Vivian's agent rejoiced that since a meeting on 16 June 'the Wesleyans have been with us to a man. I need not point out to you the vast importance of this fact.'[20] Under these circumstances, which were present to a lesser degree in earlier decades, the Conservatives had little chance of success.

The final, and at times the most decisive factor working against the Conservatives was the so-called 'Lemon connection'. The family's seat was at Carclew overlooking Restronguet Creek, south of Truro, and Sir William Lemon who was a county M.P. from 1774 until his death fifty years later seemed thoroughly representative of Cornwall's wealthy gentry. He was educated at Christchurch, Oxford, and enjoyed the educational and cultural benefits of the Grand Tour before settling down to a life of public service.[21] Prior to his 1774 victory he married Jane, daughter of James Buller of Morval, whose family had regularly held one county seat for much of the eighteenth century. The sequel was a formidable political alliance, for the Bullers were also among Cornwall's most powerful borough mongers.

Yet Lemon's grandfather had begun life as a labourer. Through a combination of talent, industry and luck he eventually became the owner of Wheal Fortune near Marazion, several mines in Gwennap, plus various commercial interests.[22] Thus in three generations the Lemons, upon whom Winston Graham's Warleggans of Carclew were based in his popular *Poldark* novels, rose from nobodies to powerful, grudgingly respected gentry.

Sir William Lemon had twelve children, his third son Charles (born 1784) inheriting his baronetcy and fortune in 1824. In the meantime two of Lemon's daughters married into longer established, more prestigious Cornish families, Harriet to Francis Basset, Baron De Dunstanville, while Caroline became the wife of John Tremayne, a highly respected county M.P. from 1806 until his retirement in 1826. The Willyams of Carnanton, the Trelawnys, Molesworths, and Aclands in neighbouring Devon were also linked by marriage to the Lemons, these attachments spreading across the political spectrum.

Of all of them the Lemon-Tremayne link was the most important. By 1826 Sir Charles Lemon's three children were dead so he eventually nominated Arthur Tremayne (born 1827) as his heir. The Tremaynes were determinedly Conservative, just as Arthur's uncle was one of Cornwall's best known Whig-Liberals. This was the crux of the 'Lemon connection'; when Sir Charles was actively involved in county politics he demanded and received the support of his Conservative relatives. For their part neither John Tremayne junior nor, in the 1860s, Arthur could hope to be elected for West Cornwall without the approval of Carclew. Rarely was it forthcoming. Even worse, as Lord Falmouth found in 1835, any other Conservative candidate running against the Liberals would receive no more than fragmentary support from his local party, at least while Sir Charles Lemon was one of the sitting members. How then did these various undercurrents affect the outcome of the five vacancies occurring between 1832 and 1868?

IV

The single Conservative breakthrough, shortlived as it was, came in 1841 when the party re-asserted its grip on county seats throughout England and Wales. Sir Charles Lemon retired less than a month before the general election, guaranteeing Lord Boscaween Rose's success. Eight months later after the death of Lord Falmouth in December 1841 and his son's elevation to the peerage, Lemon was successful at the by-election. Gash has implied that this train of events was the outcome of negotiations among Cornwall's aristocracy and gentry, but it was probably nothing of the sort.

Lemon was regarded as the representative of the agricultural interest, although like most Cornish landlords he also invested in various mining activities. Prior to the general election agriculture was suffering a periodic downturn so landlords and farmers were notably unenthusiastic about the Melbourne government's last ditch stand - the proposed introduction of a low fixed duty on imported corn. Having no illusions about the weakness of the existing Corn Laws, Lemon was in complete harmony with the government - he was a free trader. On the other hand the agriculturists whom he represented quickly made him aware of the obvious proviso to their support - Lemon would have to publicly favour the existing law. Otherwise their support and votes would go to Boscawen Rose.[23]

Lemon's vulnerability to attack by many of his constituents was exposed by a second issue. This was the proposed abolition of Church Rates. At the two preceding elections Lemon had been publicly embarassed on the hustings by criticism of his opposition to the legislation. He went to great lengths in 1837 to explain why he had voted against the government's plan to eliminate them, preferring instead a committee of enquiry. A sincere supporter of the Church of England's hegemony, and with influential friends and relatives who were similarly disinclined to agree to any erosion of the Church's finances, he faced a dilemma.[24] Complaints about the rates were rife throughout West Cornwall in 1838-40, so he was certain once again to be subjected to persistent questioning. When we consider Lemon's occasional votes with the Conservatives in 1840-41 and earlier in the mid 1830s, (proof, some believed, of the influence of his relatives) it may have been adherence to political principles which persuaded Lemon to refuse to walk the electoral tightrope between hostile dissenters and farmers. Two other events may have precipitated his retirement. These were the likelihood of his receiving a peerage in 1838, and the short-lived break-up of the 'Lemon connection'. The peerage issue came up in May, prompting Lemon to write to inform his brother-in-law Tremayne that he would not accept unless he was certain a Whig-Liberal would replace him, possibly John Basset.[25] Lemon was concerned to stop people making promises to Lord Falmouth which might preclude them from supporting Basset. The latter was told 'under a promise of strictest secrecy - and he went and told it to Lord Falmouth.'[26] No doubt this heartened the Conservative challengers just as rumours in 1840 of Lemon's retirement motivated them to press on.

The final complication was Lemon's position vis-a-vis Pendarves and his relatives and close friends. In May-June 1841 as the Melbourne government slid towards defeat and the dissolution of Parliament, friends of Lemon and Pendarves began canvassing on their behalf. On 24 May Alfred Jenkin, steward to the Robartes family of Lanhydrock in East Cornwall informed Thomas Robartes that 'Lady Basset, J.H. Tremayne, Canon Rogers etc intend to divide their influence between Lord Boscawen and Sir Chas Lemon, provided the latter does not coalesce with E.W.W. Pendarves.'[27] Lemon was not prepared to do this and one week later Jenkin noted that Lady Basset, the Duke of Leeds and Canon Rogers had all thrown their weight behind Boscawen Rose.[28] This must have been the last straw for Lemon and soon afterwards he announced his retirement, knowing he was a certainty to finish at the foot of the poll if there was a contest.

When he reluctantly resumed his political career in January-February 1842, believing John Basset was now prepared to contest the vacancy as a Conservative, Lemon took his stand on principles. Never again were there to be any doubts about his liberalism, unlike Basset's Conservatism. The latter's election committee quibbled over his proposed address and so he withdrew, despite a conviction among some observers that Lemon was still half-hearted about contesting the by-election.[29] Ultimately he had no cause for concern once Basset dropped out. According to G.W.F. Gregor, a prominent western Conservative,

> Sir Richard Vyvyan who was applied to in the first instance, continues to adhere to his resolution of not giving up Helstone, and the very few gentlemen of our party in this Division, who could have the smallest chance of success, are deterred from coming forward, from various family and other reasons; - so that Sir Charles Lemon, who has thrown himself into the arms of the Radical Party, has every chance of walking over the course.[30]

He was right; the pattern of West Cornwall politics was set for the next 27 years.

V

The 1847 general election passed uneventfully, however in 1851 the Conservatives began to stir themselves once again. Pendarves was 76 years of age and in poor health. Furthermore many of the yeomen and tenant farmers were angry at the final phasing out of agricultural protection. In East Cornwall they formed a Society for the Protection of Native Industry and in the West there was talk of starting a protectionist - John Tremayne junior - at the appropriate time. The idea may have originated with Lord Falmouth or Nicholas Kendall of Pelynt in East Cornwall.[31] Kendall had a long involvement in Conservative affairs, was energetic, outspoken and ambitious, although his social position (he was a member of the lesser gentry with a small estate) meant he was outside the circle of those who usually decided upon likely county candidates. Falmouth believed Tremayne would come forward on 'general Protectionist and Church principles,' provided his father's condition of a substantial requisition or deputation was met. Kendall was to organise this, while Falmouth agreed to secretly bear the expense, adding, 'but I will take care that my tenants have timely intimation of my wishes and intentions - and I feel sure that Lady Basset and Mr Collins will act with me, though I am not so sure of Mr Gregor, but wd fain hope he will join us.'[32] Falmouth stressed there was to be no attack on Lemon's seat, the irrevocable condition on which Tremayne senior would allow his son to stand. Therefore he could only come forward if there was a vacancy.

In the meantime Michael Williams was known to be willing to spend £10,000 to come in - as a Liberal - at a by-election. This meant that *if* Tremayne won - and the contest would be very expensive - he would then have another fight on his hands at the forthcoming general election.[33] Dr Clement Carlyon, a reliable Conservative who was privy to the local party's workings, thought that in those circumstances Sir Charles Lemon would probably persuade his nephew to stand down, leaving the Conservatives to find another candidate. Frustrated and disappointed at this apparent stalemate Carlyon bemoaned the family 'entanglement' between uncle and nephew, especially as he knew plans were afoot to establish the Conservative electoral organisation on a sound footing in West Cornwall.[34] By mid-May that idea was dead. Thus at the 1852 general election Pendarves and Lemon were re-elected.

When Pendarves, the Division's mining representative, died early the following year the vacancy discussed in 1851 became a reality. Without any fuss Michael Williams took his place, scaring off potential challengers by his preparedness to use his great wealth to set the seal on his family's respectability. With no pending general election the question then is why did the Conservatives not implement their 1851 plan, for this time Lemon's seat would have been safe? One difficulty was that Tremayne was identified with the agricultural, not the mining interest, and another was the certain expense. But overshadowing both of these was a disastrous split in Conservative ranks resulting from Nicholas Kendall's election in 1852 for East Cornwall.

Supported by many farmers still angry at the loss of agricultural protection, Kendall ostensibly ran as the second Conservative, supporting William Carew, the party's sitting member. To many people's surprise, after months of intriguing he defeated Carew, who was supported by almost all of

Cornwall's leading Conservatives - Falmouth, Tremayne, Lady Basset, Gregor, Lord St Germans, G.M. Fortescue and others. Crucially for electoral politics in West Cornwall Sir Richard Vyvyan allied himself with Kendall as did Lord Mt Edgecumbe and many of the lesser gentry.[35] A divided Conservative party was not unusual (Sir Charles Lemon's role will be recalled) but this was different. Rightly or wrongly those supporting Carew were certain they had been deceived by men whom they regarded as socially inferior, and they could not forget the humiliation of their defeat. G.M. Fortescue correctly forecast that 'the soreness that is left behind will I fear long remain . . .':[36] It reverberated through Cornwall until Kendall finally retired in 1868.

Having endured a succession of let-downs since 1841 the western Conservatives in 1857 suddenly found a ray of hope, for Sir Charles Lemon announced his retirement. Custom dictated he be replaced by an agriculturalist, so with his uncle out of the way John Tremayne junior was the party's ideal choice. What followed was an embarrassing disaster, succinctly described in the Chief Whip Sir William Jolliffe's election notebook:

> Last election Mr Williams and Mr Davey started on the Liberal interest and Mr Tremayne on the Cons. Mr Williams was favourable to Tremayne, but instead of splitting his votes with Mr Williams so as to prevent the necessity of that gentleman coalescing with Davey he solicited plumpers and asked Cons who had before supported Williams to withdraw from him. Williams whose known Cons tendencies, would have sensed (?) the arrangement placed him at the foot of the poll, was thus actually as he explained to me driven to split 1300 votes with Davey and Mr Tremayne's party, seeing the mess they had made, withdrew their candidate.[37]

However this was not the entire story.

When he announced he was standing Tremayne made it clear he was coming forward in Lemon's place at the behest of many influential friends. Soon afterwards Richard Davey, a Liberal, published an address in both county newspapers, claiming he was responding to a requisition and elaborating on his 30 year involvement in the reform struggle.[38] The pro-Conservative *Royal Cornwall Gazette* believed Davey was a most unsuitable candidate because the mining interest was already represented by Michael Williams. Even more significantly the paper acknowledged Davey was a successful mine adventurer and a man of great wealth, 'but however influential in his own business and town (Redruth), he has never taken the position or devoted himself to the duties of a county gentleman, and we know not of any pretensions he can advance to the distinguished trust of a County Member.'[39] So Davey carried with him two formidable disadvantages which should have boosted Tremayne's chances.

Enter Sir Richard Vyvyan, nemesis of the Western Conservatives. Unbeknown to all but a very few he encouraged John St Aubyn to contest the seat. However, St Aubyn demurred.[40] G.W. Gregor then asked Vyvyan to be on Tremayne's Committee. He declined, probably because of the 1852 imbroglio, then found Tremayne was contemplating being Chairman of Carew's Committee in East Cornwall (Carew was intent upon winning back 'his' seat from Kendall) and was intending to give his undivided support to Carew. Vyvyan responded by declaring his undivided support in the West would therefore go to the Liberal Michael Williams.[41] This soon became public knowledge and ruined Tremayne's chances. When he published his withdrawal he mentioned that 'some of those who still call themselves Conservatives have withdrawn from me their support in the Western Division'. Tremayne believed his chances were then 'very precarious' and to continue would only produce more bitterness and dissension 'which already exists in the Conservative party in the County'.[42] From beginning with everything in their favour, including the 'Lemon connection', the Conservatives themselves destroyed their hopes of winning the seat they so badly coveted. Not surprisingly Tremayne's name rarely came up again in discussions of prospective candidates.

The outcome of 1857 was the dominance of the mining interest, much to the consternation of the so-called 'Whig and Tory Squires' identified with agriculture. Nevertheless their state of mind improved early in mid 1858 when Michael Williams' death gave them the opportunity to come to an arrangement with a suitable representative. With their amazing propensity for bungling the Conservatives courted Williams' eldest son John Michael, another mining man. This ill-advised step was certain to antagonise the squires, who in the meantime were persuaded to back John St Aubyn.[43] Vyvyan spread the story that St Aubyn would be a loyal supporter of Lord Derby's Conservative government, when in fact he was an opponent. When J.M. Williams commenced canvassing the electorate he found that many Conservative landowners had already pledged support for St Aubyn. Even worse, the Tremayne and Lemon interests were committed to St Aubyn too.[44] No wonder J.M. Williams refused to enter the starting blocks, having no wish to be associated with another Conservative disaster. The result was the unopposed election of St Aubyn, restoring the usual balance between interests.

Never again was it to be disturbed until 1868, although the Conservatives had a final spasm of effort in 1864 when Lord Churston, one of the party's chief organisers in the South West reported to Vyvyan that William Williams was eager for his son Frederick to stand for West Cornwall. Churston found the idea appealing because Williams could be portrayed as a representative of both the mining and agricultural interests![45] Vyvyan lost no time in dashing these hopes, pointing out an often overlooked reality - the Conservatives had neglected the registers for years. With a preponderance of Methodists in West Cornwall, little landlord influence, and Williams himself known to very few in the constituency it was a waste of time and energy.[46]

Eighteen months later with the general election imminent, electoral politics in West Cornwall turned full circle. In 1835 Lord Falmouth complained of the 'Lemon connection's' impact on Conservative prospects, the direct result then being the absence of a candidate at the ensuing election. Since that time the 'connection' had been a perpetual difficulty. Now, thirty years later, it again hindered Conservative efforts. J.J. Roger, who years earlier had been regarded as a possible county member for West Cornwall, explained to Sir Richard Vyvyan:

> It would be unkind to Colonel T [Arthur Tremayne] to invite him to be a candidate on tlle 'only politics' which would make him desirable: as he could scarcely be requested to announce a ?(sic) in direct opposition to Carclew. It may well be however, that, at a future time, he might be ready to stand a contest on the right side.[47]

As always the Conservatives were desperately clutching at straws; rumours were circulating that Davey was unpopular, especially in Redruth where he had formerly enjoyed great support, and that he would retire if opposed. There was also talk of a Redruth deputation requesting Tremayne to stand, then logic overcame wishful thinking and the plans were shelved again. The one ray of hope for Rogers was the likelihood that John Tremayne, 'a very staunch Conservative', might agree to come forward again in the future![48]

VI

The Liberals' hegemony in West Cornwall between 1832 and 1868 was based upon much more than a saga of Conservative ineptitude, feuding, or stupidity. Leading Liberals built upon their natural advantages established in the 1830s, were united, and above all were quick to adapt to the politics of registration, rather than relying on the much less certain politics of influence as their opponents did. This was epitomised by their efforts in 1868 when Davey retired and the party moved quickly to nominate Pendarves Vivian, a Welsh mine-owner with strong family ties to Cornwall. Past history told the Liberals their opponents were most likely to exert themselves when a vacancy occurred, so they left nothing to chance.

From July Vivian's principal election agent S.T.G. Downing, a Redruth solicitor, began a daily stream of letters to Vivian detailing the steps to be taken to build up the register. The parishes were scoured for potential voters, great care being taken to avoid placing possible Conservatives on the list of voters. Downing knew those landlords and businessmen whose politics were Conservative and who might pressure voters over whom they had some influence.[49] Therefore, the objective he took such pains to impress on his assistants, was to avoid registering anyone who might conceivably vote against a Liberal candidate, that is, 'persons of doubtful politics'.[50] Simultaneously, Downing did not neglect the influence available to the Liberals: 'all our large properties are being worked up by the Stewards and Lord Falmouth's rental alone will show an immense number of new voters, the same may be said for

Mr Robartes' property *and* that of others.'[51] The outcome was that the Liberals successfully claimed more than two and a half times the new votes of their opponents (2762 to 1114), the Conservative figure being surprisingly large because none of the party's usual solicitors was engaged to attend to the registrations.[52]

Without elaborating further on the 1868 general election it may serve as a paradigm for both parties in mid-Victorian Cornwall. Where the Liberals were characterised by bustling activity, efficiency and painstaking preparation the Conservatives were lackadaisical, still handicapped by the same weaknesses obvious in earlier decades. While the Liberals carefully prepared for claimants' forms applying for inclusion on the register to be handed in to overseers by 20 July, their opponents were motionless.[53] Their party organisation was united, and both St Aubyn and Vivian were attuned to the mood of the electorate. From all sides they were told the Wesleyans were totally supporting them - principally because the election was dominated by a massive wave of nonconformist approval for Gladstone's disestablishment plan.[54]

Nevertheless, it would be quite wrong to leave an impression of a Conservative party completely moribund in West Cornwall. Between the First and Second Reform Acts four of Cornwall's seven Parliamentary boroughs were in the West - St Ives, Helston, Penryn and Falmouth and Truro. St Ives, for example, always elected Conservatives between 1832 and 1868 as did Helston from 1832 to 1857 and again from 1859 to 1865. Conservatives more than held their own in the other two boroughs too, proving the party was healthily alive, despite the dominance of Methodism and their own inherent weaknesses. Unfortunately for them, the Cornish Conservatives adopted a 'win by default' strategy, demonstrating a remarkable reluctance to become involved in registrations or contests, probably because of the expense. Combined with the ramifications of the ubiquitous 'Lemon connection' and behind the scenes machinations they ultimately condemned themselves to political ineffectiveness for almost forty years.

REFERENCES

1.   [B]ritish [M]useum [L]ibrary, Add. Ms 40409, fo.19, Falmouth to Peel, 1 January, 1835.
2.   Ibid., fo.20.
3.   Ibid., fos.20-21.
4.   Norman Gash, *Politics in the Age of Peel*, New York, 1971, p. 191.
5.   W.B. Elvins, 'The Reform Movement and County Politics in Cornwall 1809-1852' (unpublished M.A. thesis, University of Birmingham, 1959), ch.7, pp. 11-16. This excellent study contains a wealth of information on various aspects of West Cornwall electoral politics to 1842.
6.   J. Vincent & M. Stenton (eds.), *McCalmont's Parliamentary Poll Book. British Election Results 1832-1918*, Brighton, 1971, p. 70. Table 1 is compiled from this source.
7.   Biographical information on Pendarves, Williams and Davey is from C.G. Boase, *Collectanea Cornubiensia. A Collection of Biographical and Topographical Notes Relating to the County of Cornwall*, Truro, 1890, and Michael Stenton, *Who's Who of British Members of Parliament*, Vols I, II, Hassocks, 1976-78.
8.   Sir L. Namier and J. Brooke, *The House of Commons 1754-90*, Vol.II, London, 1964 p. 102.

9.   Philip Payton, *The Making of Modern Cornwall. Historical Experience and the Persistence of 'Difference'*, Redruth, 1992, pp. 56-7 and pp. 87-91.
10. Payton, 1992, p. 56.
11. Antony House, (Cornwall), Carew Mss. CC/63/7 September (?) 1832.
12. Ibid., correspondence between Pole Carew and Jefferey, March & April 1833.
13. [C]ornwall [R]ecord [O]ffice, Vyvyan Mss, DD.V. 22M/BO/36/46 Sir Richard Vyvyan to Lord Churston, 6 January, 1864.
14. Ibid., 24/9 John Vivian to Vyvyan, 10 September, 1832.
15. *British Parliamentary Papers*, Numbers of Electors, 1833, XXVII; 1834, IX; 1836, XLIII; 1837-38, XLIV; 1844, (2) XXXVIII.
16. Royal Cornwall Gazette, 18 October 1839
17. C.R.O., Vyvyan Mss. op.cit., Vyvyan to Churston and to W. Williams, 6 January, 1864.
18. Peter Hayden, 'Culture, Creed and Conflict: Methodism and Politics in Cornwall, c.1832-1979' (unpublished Ph.D. thesis, University of Liverpool, 1982), p. 56.
19. C.R.O., Pendarves Vivian Mss, DO.PU (290) 1, A.P. Vivian to John St Aubyn, (copy), 27 June, 1868.
20. Ibid., T.S.G. Downing to Vivian, 14 July, 1868.
21. Elvins, 1959, ch.l, p. 6 and Namier and Brooke, 1964, Vol.III, p. 64.
22. Boase, 1890, co.488 and Elvins, 1959, ch.l, p. 6.
23. Elvins, 1959, ch.8, p. 22.
24. For example, see *West Briton*, 11 August 1837
25. C.R.O., Tremayne Mss, DD.T 2810/1/2, Sir Charles Lemon to Joh Tremayne, 18 May, 1838.
26. Ibid., 22 May, 1838.
27. Royal Institution of Cornwall, Jenkin Letterbooks, H.J/1/19, A. Jenkin to T.J. Agar-Roberts, 24 May, 1841.
28. Ibid., Jenkin to A.M. Agar, 1 June, 1841.
29. Ibid., Jenkin to T.J. Agar-Robartes, 6, 10, 19, 22, 24 Januarv, 1842.
30. B.M.L., Add Ms 4051, fo.130, G.W.F. Gregor to Sir Robert Peel 29 January, 1842.
31. Pelynt (Cornwall), Kendall Mss, Dr Clement Carlyon to Nicholas Kendall, 26 March, 1851.
32. Ibid..
33. Ibid., 7 April, 1851.
34. Ibid and Kendall to Carlyon 5 April 1851.
35. Ibid., Francis Glanville to Kendall, 26 May, 1852, and other correspondence March to August, 1852.
36. Devon Record Office, Acland of Broadclyst Mss, 1148 M/Box8/4 Fortescue to Sir Thomas Acland, 24 July, 1852.
37. [S]omerset [R]ecord [O]ffice, Hylton Mss, DD/HY/24/23, Election Notebook 1859, part 1, 'West Cornwall'.
38. *Royal Cornwall Gazette*, 20 and 27 March 1857. Tremayne's was issued on 11 March, Davey's on 19 March.
39. Ibid., 20 March 1857. The paper added. 'Mr Davey is most respectable in his place, but when he seeks a high trust to which his chief claim must be the wealth he has amassed, ... he forgets both himself, and the recognized proprieties of social and political distinctions.'
40. C.R.O. Vyvyan Mss DD. V 22M/Bo/36/46 Vyvyan to Thomas Tyacke, 26 May, 1858.
41. Pelynt (Cornwall), Kendall Mss, Vyvyan to Kendall 31 March, 1857.
42. *Roval Cornwall Gazette*, 3 April 1857.
43. S.R.O. Hylton Mss, DD/HY/24/17/40, Samuel Triscott to Sir William Jolliffe, 23 June, 1858.
44. Ibid., 15 June, 1858.
45. C.R.0. Vyvyan Mss, 22M/BQ/36/46, Churston to Vyvyan 4 January, 1864.
46. Ibid., Vyvyan to Churston, 6 January, 1864.
47. Ibid., Rogers to Vyvyan, 5 June, 1865.
48. Ibid., 13 June, 1865.
49. C.R.0., Pendarves Vivian Mss, DD. PV (290) 1, Downing to Vivian, 10 & 15 July, 1868.
50. Ibid., 15 July, 1868.
51. Ibid., 6 July, 1868. The sixth Viscount Falmouth was a Liberal.
52. Ibid., H.M. Grylls to Vivian, 19 August, 1868.

53.   Ibid., see Downing's correspondence with Vivian from 8 to 25 July, 1868.
54.   Ibid., for example Downing to Vivian, 14 July, 1868.

'BLUE BOOKS'
AS SOURCES FOR CORNISH EMIGRATION
HISTORY
Margaret James-Korany

INTRODUCTION

The paradoxical quip that maintains 'They cannot know Cornwall who only Cornwall know' indicates how essential emigration and the colonisation of distant lands were to the Cornish identity. The concept of emigration as somehow a naturally accepted and on-going phenomenon formed an integral part of the Cornish psyche. In the mid-nineteenth and early twentieth centuries there was probably no Cornish family which did not have at least one relative or close friend who was 'away', who had emigrated somewhere. Any social historian of Cornwall must take emigration into account, for the emigrant tide not only put its marks on the new lands, but also left complex social, cultural and economic traces on the Cornish homeland. Expressions such as 'Cousin Jacks and Cousin Jennies', 'Birds of Passage', 'Remittances', 'gone 'Merica' conjure up enduring images and memories in most Cornish minds. The influence of remittances on the Cornish economy and society is a subject for research in its own right. Thousands of women were left to head families and bring them up alone. This absence of many fathers bred a special matriarchal strength, hard to measure, in working class society in Cornwall. Emigrants' stories and letters provided windows on the wider world and fostered a world view different from that of societies where emigration was not so prevalent, a view of the world where North America, for example, was 'the next parish'.

The historian focusing on emigration can make innumerable hypotheses based on various forms of qualitative evidence such as: family histories, local newspaper entries, reports and editorials, and secondary sources of many kinds, but sooner or later he/she needs numbers, needs to quantify. Where can the historian of Cornish emigration find such quantifiable evidence?

This author's interest was concentrated primarily on Cornish emigration to Canada, especially during the early period from the end of the Napoleonic Wars until the mid-nineteenth century (1815-1860), the period of 'The Great

31

To Sail the First of April,

1841,.

FOR QUEBEC,

The fine fast sailing, British-built, Copper bolted BARQUE

VITTORIA,

650 Tons Burthen,

Mosey Simpson, Commander,

LYING AT MALPUS, IN TRURO RIVER,

Has very superior accommodation for Steerage and Cabin Passengers.

The Commander having been many years in the North American Trade, can give much valuable information regarding the Colonies, to any that may feel disposed to take a passage in the said ship.

Apply to the CAPTAIN on board,

Mrs. SIMPSON, at the Seven Stars Inn, Truro ,

Or to the Owner, NICHOLAS MITCHELL, Malpus.

Dated, February 13th, 1841.

E. HEARD, PRINTER, BOOKBINDER, &c., BOSCAWEN-STREET, TRURO.

Migration' in Canada. This was virtually virgin historical territory, rather like the virgin frontier land itself to which many Cornish pioneers went. We wanted to know approximately how many Cornish emigrants from which parts of Cornwall had taken part in this primarily agricultural 'Great Migration'. Scottish and Irish emigrants were other large Celtic groups who participated more numerously in this migratory movement than did the Cornish. Consideration of their role in the development of Canada has been facilitated not only by their numbers, but also by the fact that Scottish and Irish emigrants were always mentioned and calculated separately in official documents, counted as separate ethnic groups. Cornish emigrants, like the Welsh, were always counted inside English statistics, a fact oft-lamented by Cornish historians. And despite the fact that tell-tale Cornish surnames could occasionally act as indicators of a Cornish presence, the counting of surnames on land or township rolls in foreign lands can be nothing more than that, merely hints or indicators, and can in no way replace general statistics.

BLUE BOOKS AS SOURCES OF QUANTITATIVE DATA

But the problem can be got around. Hidden away among the thousands of *Parliamentary Sessional Papers* of the British government are documents which, until the Second World War, were colloquially called Blue Books. Blue Books is not an official term, the librarian will explain, but was used to denote papers on subjects concerning external relations, diplomacy and colonies, emigration included. Blue Books were originally bound in blue covers and many were command papers (ordered to be printed by the Monarch and presented before both Houses of Parliament). Using the *British Parliamentary Papers General Index*, a variety of these Blue Books covering the middle decades of the nineteenth century were consulted for the study described in this paper. They contained colonial government reports and colonial correspondence on various topics both general and specific, and later the *General Reports of the Colonial Lands and Emigration Commissioners*. They are primary sources providing a wide range and vast quantity of both quantitative and qualitative data. A researcher must be ready, however, to accept that their examination will be time-consuming, for their titles and form often vary from administration to administration and sometimes from year to year. Moreover, the same type of information was often included under documents of differing names, and the statistics often contained many inconsistencies.

But, by determined scrutiny, it was possible to compile what was needed most: statistics of the numbers of emigrants arriving in Quebec each year from 1831 to 1860 from individual ports in Britain, including of course Cornish ports (Table 2). These statistics do not count those going to the Maritime Provinces of British North America, namely Prince Edward Island, Nova Scotia, New Brunswick or Newfoundland,[1] but only those to the Province of Canada proper. There were also statistics for the earlier years 1825-1830[2] (Table 1) but these statistics were for all the colonies of British North America, that is, Canada and the Maritime colonies. These early years are more incomplete because the counting of emigrants was something almost incidental to trade at this time. But with year of departure and port of departure as the two axes, the matrices could be completed.

TABLE 1
NUMBER OF PERSONS WHO EMIGRATED FROM SELECTED
PORTS TO BRITISH NORTH AMERICA 1825-30

PORT OF DEPARTURE	1825	1826	1827	1828	1829	1830
PLYMOUTH	45	25	32	17	82	476
BIDEFORD		31	13			
FALMOUTH						
PADSTOW					102	171
PENZANCE						
LONDON	493	363	456	408	349	616

Information taken from Parliamentary Sessional Papers 1833 Vol. XXVI p.279.

Thus by delving into annual reports of emigration compiled in Britain, and emigration agents' reports from the colonies, the statistics for the Cornish ports mentioned in the lists were extracted. These were the ports of Padstow, StIves, Penzance, Falmouth, Truro and Fowey. To these purely Cornish ports had to be added the ports of Bideford and Plymouth.

Bideford was added because it was the natural and traditional port of embarkation for a large number of parishes in North Cornwall, parishes such as Morwenstow, Kilkhampton, Launcells, Bridgerule, Marhamchurch . . ., the whole area straddling the border with North Devon where the Tamar no longer made an effective dividing line. These parishes of North Devon and North Cornwall made a geographically and in certain respects socio-culturally homogeneous area, a relatively poor and isolated district that also provided,

TABLE 2
EMIGRANT ARRIVALS AT QUEBEC AND MONTREAL
FROM PORTS OF EMBARKATION FOR CORNISH EMIGRANTS

	Plymouth	Bideford	Padstow	Fowey	Truro	Falmouth	Penzance	St Ives	TOTAL
1831	474	51	5			77	19		626
1832	1398	60	335			107	28		1928
1833	440		53			31			524
1834	850		29			59	12		950
1835	211		13				13		237
1836	88	16	8			11			123
1837	403		1			3	1		408
1838	35	8	1			17			61
1839	58		9						67
1840	119	26	242			3	1		391
1841	241	164	558				15	19	997
1842	1207	142	1173	233		195	7	90	3047
1843	769	468	271	65	7		10		1590
1844	381	72	215		164		60		892
1845	656	109	482		155		144		1546
1846	617	119	296	12		32	150	73	1299
1847	1121	24	646		101	211	66	63	2232
1848	1590	57	428	3	73	215	232	108	2706
1849	1628	176	520	122	151	314	15	106	3032
1850	1049	94	201	257	69	83		21	1774
1851	1761	222	325	133		44			2485
1852	1534	219	306	95	14	23			2191
1853	1495	190	30	169					1884
1854	2701	1	8	320	2	46			3078
1855	2026	46	14	132	52				2270
1856	1673	16	13		163	35			1900
1857	2805		16	70	37		5		2933
1858	538				49				587
1859	166				6		6		178
1860	110								110
TOTAL	28144	2280	6198	1611	1043	1506	782	480	42046

importantly for this particular research, the birth-place of the Bible Christian movement which was to play such an important role in encouraging and funnelling networks of emigrants into Canada and the Maritime provinces of British North America. In a sense, the remote extremities of north-western Devon were part of a 'Greater Cornwall'.

Plymouth was included for two main reasons. Firstly, Plymouth was the natural port of embarkation for a large part of south-east Cornwall; and secondly, boats recorded in Quebec as sailing from Plymouth had often stopped off at Cornish ports, especially Falmouth, but also Penzance, to pick up West Cornwall emigrants, who on occasions made up at least half the passengers. Having to accept that it would be almost impossible to know what proportion of emigrants from Bideford and Plymouth each year were strictly Cornish, emigrants from these two ports had nonetheless to be counted in. These statistics, then, come from a combination of emigration agents' reports from Canada and the *General Reports of the Colonial Land and Emigration Commissioners*. These statistics did not always tally, and try as one may, they can never of course be 100% accurate. One can only note inconsistencies, try to explain them, and take them into account. Sometimes numbers quoted in the emigration agents' reports are at slight variance with the final official printing of statistics by the government. Various factors explain this. Sometimes only steerage passengers are counted, sometimes steerage and cabin passengers. Only sometimes are infant babies counted. Numbers of emigrants from Cornish ports are almost certainly higher than those officially indicated, as for much of the period there was an official emigration agent in Plymouth but none in the whole of Cornwall. Not all those who left as emigrants were counted as such. Emigration boats were often family concerns and many emigrants would have been known to the crew. Some may have partially worked their way across the Atlantic. The numerous inlets on fairly isolated stretches of the Cornish coast, so widely used for smuggling brandy and tobacco, could just as easily have smuggled extra emigrants aboard, as Helen Cowan[3] has suggested.

Moreover, these statistics do not include the (probably few) Cornish emigrants who left in the 1840s and 1850s from Liverpool and London. But occasional advertisements can be found in Cornish newspapers for agents of Liverpool ships together with fares from Cornish ports to Liverpool.[4] After the 1850s of course, Liverpool, with a regular steamship service, was to become the important port of departure for Cornish emigrants to Canada and the United States (US). Nor, of course, can these statistics count the numbers of Cornish who came to Canada via the New York route, or discount the Cornish emigrants going straight to the US via the St Lawrence route (e.g. miners going to the mines of the US part of Lake Superior). Nor do the 1831-1860 statistics count those (probably few) who voyaged to one of the 'Lower' ports of the Maritime colonies (Halifax or Charlottetown, for example) before moving up the St Lawrence to Canada on another ship. These latter factors are problems common to historians of emigration in general, and are not peculiar to studies of Cornish emigration.

But if anything these statistics probably provide a conservative estimate of Cornish emigration. We find advertisements in Cornish newspapers for emigrants for boats sailing from Helford, Charlestown, or Boscastle.[5] Did these emigrants ever get counted on the other side or in official statistics? As Helen Cowan has suggested, in remoter areas with smaller ports, emigrants could have left in small trading vessels without anyone knowing. With no government emigration agent immediately to hand, purely Cornish ports were ideally suited to this kind of trade. Yet while accepting all these limitations and imperfections, the statistics do provide valuable indicators of general trends and widen the lens on to a more whole picture of emigration to Canada. Immediately, certain general hypotheses either suggested themselves, seemed to be confirmed or were put in question by these figures. Firstly, we could estimate that in the period from 1831 to 1860 at least 42,000 emigrants, probably more, left Cornwall and the border areas of Devon for the Province of Canada. Almost all would go to Upper Canada (i.e. Canada West or Ontario as it was successively known). After a 'kick-start' surge of 1928 emigrants in 1832, the flood years from 1842 to 1857 consistently sent emigrants in the one, two or three thousands each year from the area. But how many leaked sooner or later across the border to become part of the wider American immigration, we could not tell.

The 'fashion' for emigration to Canada, begun in the 1820s everywhere in Britain as a reaction to the economic, particularly agricultural, hardship following the end of the Napoleonic Wars, seems to have reached a first peak in 1832 in Cornwall. It slowed down by the mid 1830s as news of disturbances and unrest and talk of reform, and then news of the rebellions in Upper and Lower Canada in 1837-38, reached back home surprisingly fast through returning sailors, letters and missionary reports in religious journals (for example, the *Bible Christian Journal*). Emigration picked up again with a vengeance during the 'hungry'' 1840s and what had been primarily a phenomenon of North and East Cornwall, spread to include West Cornwall in increasing numbers. Emigration to Canada tapered off rapidly in the late 1850s, so that by the end of that decade immigration from Cornwall was negligible. Indeed, emigration from the British Isles to Canada generally had dwindled from a tide to a dribble, at least temporarily.

Of the purely Cornish ports serving exclusively Cornish emigrants, Padstow was by far the biggest and most regular sender of emigrants and probably the best indicator of the particular situation in North Cornwall. Padstow sent approximately 6200 emigrants to Canada in the 1831-1860 period. It would appear that the emigrant trade from Padstow began in 1829 and continued until 1857. There is an entry for every year of that period; even during the difficult years of the Rebellions (1837-1838) one emigrant is recorded leaving each year. In 1841 Padstow was the third highest English emigrant port for Canada (Cornish ports being tabulated as English), sending 558 emigrants. Liverpool was first with 2994, but London sent only 642 that year and Padstow's 558 emigrants was much greater than Plymouth's 241. 1842 was a bumper year for emigration from Cornwall. Padstow with its 1,173 emigrants to Canada that year was again the third most important port. It was only just beaten by Plymouth with 1,207. First, of course, was Liverpool with its 5,823 emigrants, but Padstow sent more than London (1035).

There is a probability that Fowey[6] boats brought some emigrants to Canada before the 1842 start date in the statistics above, emigrants that for some reason were not counted officially. Perhaps further investigation may be able to prove this. Certainly, there are some advertisements in Cornish newspapers for emigrant boats from Fowey during this early period. As early as June 1819 there was an advertisement in the *West Briton* which read 'For Quebec. The brig Sceptre of 154 tons from Fowey. Apply to Mr. Borlase at the Ship Inn, Fowey' and specified passenger fares. Yet the matrix indicates that Fowey with a start in the bumper 1842 year of 233 emigrants, came into its own as a regular emigrant port from 1849 through to the mid 1850s. This coincides with what is indicated in Canadian sources, that closely-knit groups from the parishes around Fowey, such as Pelynt, mainly Bible Christians and other Methodists, sailed from Fowey and moved into specific areas of Upper Canada in groups in the early 1850s.

As emigration became more commonplace, shipping agents became more adept at spreading their nets wider. Ships from Plymouth picked up Falmouth or Penzance passengers quite regularly. Hence large numbers of the passengers in the Plymouth statistics were in fact passengers who embarked at West Cornwall ports.[7] This applied especially during the 1850s when there were very few emigrants (at least official ones) sailing direct from Falmouth, Truro, St Ives or Penzance for Quebec.

It was thus the search for Cornish emigration statistics that originally took us to these Blue Books with their valuable data for this period of Cornish emigration to Canada, but it was soon realised that many of these documents could very profitably be used by those studying Cornish emigration generally, or emigration to other areas. Just one example: anyone interested in Cornish emigration to Australia or South Africa might be concerned to use the statistics provided in the 1850 General Report entitled 'Return Showing the Counties whence Government Emigrants were Selected and Numbers Taken from each between 1846 and 1850'. The figures for Cornwall have been extracted, and are presented on the next page (TABLE 3).

Of all the counties of the United Kingdom, Cornwall was that with by far the most government emigrants leaving for South Australia for each of the five years considered. Cornwall sent a total of 4775 souls, of whom 3849 were adults, during the whole five-year period. Middlesex came a distant second, a long way behind with a total of 1412 souls, 1215 adults. Devon was third with a total of 1026 souls, 822 adults. Cornwall's 4775 souls were a good third of the total 14020 souls for the whole of 'England' during that period, and a good quarter of the total 17750 souls sent as government emigrants to South Australia from the whole of the UK, including those whose county of origin was not noted. These numbers suggest the economic and cultural influence the Cornish would have in Australia, and in the 'Little Cornwalls' (so well portrayed by Philip

TABLE 3
NUMBERS AND DESTINATIONS OF EMIGRANTS SELECTED FROM CORNWALL 1846-50

DESTINATION	1846 "souls"	1846 adults	1847 "souls"	1847 adults	1848 "souls"	1848 adults	1849 "souls"	1849 adults	1850 "souls"	1850 adults	TOTAL "souls"	TOTAL adults
Sydney					384	302½	227	186½	41	35½	652	524½
Victoria					817	657½	463	376½	18	15½	1298	1049½
South Australia	422	348	1563	1246	1861	1501	661	528	268	226	4775	3849
Van Dieman Land											0	0
Cape of Good Hope			11	9½	7	6	48	43½	20	17½	86	76½
Western Australia									2	2	2	2
FIVE YEAR TOTAL	422	348	1574	1255½	3069	2467	1399	1134½	349	296½		

Payton in his writings[8]) that they managed to create. Moreover, Cornwall sent a grand total of 6813 souls abroad as government emigrants during this period, between a quarter and a fifth of the 'English' total of 31,693 souls. Cornwall sent by far the largest number of government emigrants of any county during this period. If nothing else, this confirms the importance of emigration generally for Cornwall in the mid-nineteenth century.

The poor are those who leave least traces on history, yet the poor can never be ignored by the historian of emigration. It is in this context that the statistics from the 1848 Report which provide 'An Account of Persons who have been aided in Emigration from England and Wales under the Provisions of the Poor Law Amendment Act' can prove useful. The statistics for Cornish parishes involved have been extracted, but it would be very easy to employ the full set of statistics to compare Cornwall's use of the process with that of other counties of England or Wales.

These statistics reveal that the Cornish parishes were on the whole reluctant and slow to use this emigration-aid system to deal with the problems of poverty. They might have started in 1836 or 1837, but parish aid to emigrate reached its rapid peak in 1841-42 in Cornwall when 10 parishes used the scheme to aid in all 69 emigrants. From 1843 the system dwindled rapidly. Cornwall was not a big user of this form of relief; the total of 260 aided emigrants for the decade is not a large figure. But neither did Cornwall have any big landowner/ philanthropist schemes to send large groups of emigrants, unlike some areas of Scotland and Ireland and some counties of England. We hear the occasional story of an individual being helped or collected for, and mining captains sometimes took their own men with them, but generally, the individualistic Cornish practised self-help in the form of individual kinship and friendship networks to sponsor most of the Cornish emigration, at least to North America.

Of the total 260 parish-aided emigrants for this period, 123 went to Canada, 70 to Australia and 67 to New Zealand. There is no overall pattern regarding which areas of Cornwall aided emigration to which colony, but certain aspects can be noticed. None of the parishes of West Cornwall (west of the line running along the Fal to Truro and then across to the north shore at St Agnes) sent any emigrants (except Newlyn which sent six in the bumper year of 1842 to Van Dieman's Land). Another huge block of central parishes with Bodmin at its centre, stretching from Fowey to Tintagel and Probus to St Cleer took virtually no part in the scheme. Parishes along the north coast, St Agnes, Perranzubuloe, St Eval and St Merryn, together with St Columb Major inland between them, aided emigration only to Canada, and that almost entirely during the lean years of 1842 and 1843. St Columb Major aided by far the most emigrants of any Cornish parish; 44 were aided to emigrate to Canada during 1842 and 1843. Parishes of North and East Cornwall, closer to the border with Devon, were more varied in the destinations of their emigrants. Varied too was the monetary aid given the paupers to emigrate. The five from St Agnes who received 12 pounds each to go to Canada in 1840 would appear exceedingly lucky compared to the eight from St Germans who only received 17 shillings and sixpence each to go to the same destination in 1842, or to the 12 from Altarnun who received only 11 shillings and eight pence each to go to South Australia in 1845.

Other statistics can prove useful. The trans-Atlantic crossing has gone down in history as the epitome of a horrendous nightmare for nineteenth-century British emigrants, a 'crossing' where death was a very real possibility. Dangerous it certainly was, with its storms, fogs, icebergs, disease and starvation. But 'Deaths at Sea' statistics show what a low death rate and good record for relative health and cleanliness Cornish ships had in general. For example, Chief Emigration Agent Buchannan at Quebec, in his report on the 1847 emigration season, calculated mortality rates from various parts of Britain into Quebec:

Mortality from English ports (excluding Liverpool) was	1%
Mortality from German ports was	1.2%
Mortality from Scottish ports was	3.12%
Mortality from Irish ports (including Liverpool) was	10.49%
Mortality from the port of Liverpool was	15.9%
Mortality from the port of Cork was	18.73%

When we extract the death statistics for our group of ports for Cornish emigrants we find only 5 deaths for the whole year (2 from Padstow and 3 from Plymouth). Out of a total of 2232 passengers, their mortality rate was only 0.22%. For Cornish emigrants the news and stories heard about 'the crossing' would not have been as bad as those heard by Irish emigrants for whom the crossing was a nightmare indeed. Although momentous in individual families' lives, emigration, and the crossing as part of it, became accepted as a normal phenomenon in Cornish society.[9]

One of the biggest virtues of these Blue Book statistics, then, for the historian with Cornish concerns, is that they are sometimes specific enough to give statistics for individual ports, or individual sailings, or for individual counties, or even individual parishes. It is then that one can separate Cornwall from England or compare Cornwall with other counties.

BLUE BOOKS AS SOURCES OF QUALITATIVE EVIDENCE
The Blue Books are an invaluable, unique source of general statistics for numbers of emigrants leaving Cornish ports each year during the 1830s, 1840s and 1850s. These documents are also, however, excellent sources of qualitative evidence. For example, statements in the logbook of the Chief emigration officer of Canada, A.C. Buchannan, stationed in the port of Quebec, can be very revealing. For the week ending 23rd May 1840 he notes 'In the Clio from Padstow were 146 very respectable people; they are all going to settle in the Township of Whitby and near Port Hope in Upper Canada.' The word 'all' is important in that it confirms the clannishness of the Cornish and their probable

concentrations in these areas in numbers possibly large enough to recreate 'Little Cornwalls' in Canada. They were also people of means, capable of taking up land for themselves, the ideal, solid, 'respectable' pioneering settlers. Buchannan records that on September 16th of that year the same 'Clio' from Padstow, under Captain Brown, (making its second crossing that year as it nearly always did), arrived with 58 emigrants on board, 24 males, 10 females and 24 children. He comments:

> The passengers in the Clio from Padstow . . . are chiefly mechanics and farmers; a few of the former remain in Montreal for employment, the remainder are going to the townships of Aspadel (sic) and Darlington in the Newcastle District and Whitby in the Home District; they all possess sufficient means to enable them to settle on their own lands, and have friends and relations already settled in that part of the country

Buchannan was an eyewitness. His statements not only confirm for us the major areas into which Cornish emigrants were going (neighbouring Townships of Asphodel, Darlington and Whitby in this latter case) but are further hard evidence of the networking in progress between areas of Cornwall and patches of immigration into Canada through kinship and neighbourhood contacts. As such, Buchannan's statements are crucial evidence.

That emigrants, especially first generation emigrants, should be clannish and use friendship and kinship networks wherever they went is basic human nature and a useful tactic for one's physical, economic, and psychological survival. The experience of Cornish emigrants appears to have epitomised this phenomenom, as the concept of 'Cousin Jacks and Cousin Jennies' seems to imply. Justifiably, historians of emigration are increasingly interested in recreating these networks over space and time, down to the micro-scale. History 'from the bottom up' is very apt for emigration studies.

Surprisingly enough, these Blue Books can sometimes provide information on this micro-scale for historians of Cornish emigration. For example, at the 'the bottom up' end of research on Cornish emigration to Canada a file index has been compiled for every emigrant person or family who falls anywhere in the category of Cornish emigrant to Canada. Some of the names are just that, names. One such name was 'John Carthew' - anonymous until he appeared in a list of people acquiring land in Canada. He had been a lieutenant in the Royal Navy, and thus had the right to take up land on half pension. By Order of Council in 1832 he had taken up 500 acres of land (Concessions 9 and 10 of Lot 17 and Concession 10 in Lot 16 East) in Medonte Township in the Home District of Upper Canada on condition that he reside in the colony at least two years and perform his settlement duties (land clearance, agriculture, building a dwelling). He appeared on a list beside many other discharged military men taking up land in Medonte, and that he was one of only two people on this list with anywhere near 500 acres. Thus he must have carried certain weight or influence in the area, or have been able afterwards to sell off or rent his land in parcels for profit. And so now, thanks to the Blue Books, John Carthew is more than just a name.

In 'Papers Relative to Emigration' for 1849 and 1850, in the sections on South Australia, we find lists of emigrants who have bought Crown Lands in Australia, and lists of emigrants in Australia who want to sponsor other emigrants. When we extract the obviously Cornish entries we glimpse the occupational variety of Cornish people being sponsored by relatives or friends in South Australia and see in action the kinship and friendship networks that funnelled them into South Australia. Miners, of course, are well-represented. Henry Williams applied to sponsor the Paulls of Carnkie, Illogan; Richard aged 38, miner, his wife Mary Ann aged 32, and their six children ranging in age from 14 to four. John Row and John Mayor sponsored Benjamin Row, 30, a miner from Chestwater (sic) in Gwennap parish and his 29-year-old wife, Mary. The entry adds 'In the event of the death of any of the persons named, or of their being unwilling to emigrate, applicants would wish to substitute the names of Margaret and Mary Long, residing at East Wheal Rose, parish of Newland (sic) Cornwall'. Nobody, it seems, wanted to waste the chance to sponsor people from back home. Masons too are well-represented. Richard Johns sponsored James Johns, 33, mason, and his wife Mary Ann, of Copperhouse, Hayle. Peter Rowe sponsored the Rowe family of St Keverne; William, 32, mason, his wife Jane 30, and their four young children. Farmers, too, emigrated. John Broad paid 11 pounds for the passage of Margaret Broad, 54, farmer's wife of Cornwall.

Often one can read between the lines of these bald statements on official lists and try to recreate the human realities behind them. Sometimes a son settled in Australia and brought his ageing or widowed parents out to join him. William Martin paid 11 pounds for the passage of Grace Martin, 59, widow of Alternun. James Mitchell paid 22 pounds for the passage of William Mitchell, 62, farm labourer and Mary Mitchell, 58, of Alternun. Sometimes the desire to escape poverty or better oneself and one's family is abundantly clear. Malachi Deeble, on the basis of having paid 125 pounds for land, wished to apply for emigrant passages for Eliza Deeble, 17, domestic servant; James Deeble, 15, miner; and Elizabeth Deeble, 13, domestic servant, all of Callington. Another entry states that John Scoble had paid 80 pounds in November 1848 and had applied in July 1849 for emigrant passage for his sister-in-law, Mary Belman and her two children, William, five, and an infant, all of St Cleer parish. A note adds that the applicant's sister-in-law wishes to come out with her parents, whose passages will be paid. Occasionally the Blue Books allow us to follow family stories, year by year. We learn that in 1848 Francis Trezise and W.H. Roscrow bought Lot 2779, Section 84, 80 acres, with a bid of 80 pounds, one shilling. In the report af the following year we find Henry Roscrow applying for passages for William Roscrow (seven), Elizabeth Roscrow (five) and Thomas Roscrow (one), all of Camborne, on the grounds that he has paid 80 pounds, one shilling for land.

CONCLUSION

So from the micro-history story of Mr. Roscrow and his Camborne family to the general statistics on emigration from British ports, these Blue Books contain a whole range of useful data both quantitative and qualitative for Cornish history, data that may have been overlooked until now. This article has considered only a portion of what might be available in that it has discussed some two decades of these government documents and has extracted only some examples of the data on offer. A major research task might be the selection, editing and commentary of a selection of these documents pertaining to things Cornish in a form that would make them more accessible to local researchers.

In the contemporary context of increasing integration within Europe, it is important to consider Cornwall as a region in its own right with its own historical and cultural identity. Cornwall's emigration experience is a major element of that identity. A consideration and analyis of government Blue Books is certainly one valuable source for the eventual piecing together of a general picture of Cornish emigration, a picture which can then be juxtaposed with that of other emigrant groups. One might then compare emigration from Cornwall with emigration from other areas of Britain, or other areas of Europe, noting and providing explanations for the similarities and differences. One might even throw the net wider and apply the Cornish emigrant experience to more general emigration theories.[10] Migration and emigration are subjects that belong to macro-history. They go back beyond history proper into epic tale and myth. The movement of ethnic groups and the setting-up of new colonies are amongst the oldest epic themes. Intriguingly, more recently historians have been able to see these themes not only as history of *la longue durée*, macro-history, but also as micro-history. Moreover, in the global village in which we live, interest in migration and emigration studies at both micro- and macro- levels is not likely to decrease in the near future.

REFERENCES

1.   The pioneering role of the Cornish in the Maritime Provinces has been underestimated, although Basil Greenhill and Ann Giffard's book *Westcountrymen in Prince Edward's Isle: a fragment of the great migration*, Newton Abbot, 1967, begins to recognise that many Cornish left the port of Bideford.

2.   *Parliamentary Sessional Papers*, 1833 Vol. XXVI, p. 279

3.   Helen Cowan, *British Emigration to British North America*, Toronto, 1961.

4.   For example, an advertisement in the *West Briton* of 28 February 1845 offers Liverpool as a port of emigration for the Cornish, suggesting it might be cheaper even with the fare from Hayle to Liverpool at about 10 shillings. It names Mr. Edwards, auctioneer of Camborne, as Cornish agent.

5.   For example, *West Briton* of 17 July 1846 indicates that the 'Countess of Durham' would sail from Helford for Quebec around the 23rd July. *West Briton* of 12 July 1850 notes that the fast-sailing brig 'Dew Drop' would sail from Boscastle about July 15th.

6.   See also C.H. Ward-Jackson, *Ships and Shipbuilders of a Westcountry Seaport: Fowey 1786-1939*, Truro, 1986.

7.   Sometimes we are fortunate enough to be able to follow a ship's fortunes by having both the account of its sailing from Cornwall in Cornish newspapers and the Emigration Agent,

Buchanan's record of its arrival in Quebec in the Blue Books. This was the case in 1848 when Buchanan recorded the 'Lady Peel' out of Plymouth arriving with 250 emigrants (the 10 infants and 4 cabin passengers were mentioned but not included in the total) on May 21st 1848. The next day the 'Roslyn Castle' arrived from Plymouth with 205 passengers plus 16 infants and 1 cabin passenger. The *West Briton* had already recorded the sailing of these two ships, both on April 6th. The 'Lady Peel' had sailed from Penzance after 86 adults and 48 children had embarked from that region 'making with persons that had previously been taken on board at Plymouth 258 steerage and 5 cabin passengers'. The Penzance contingent was thus just over half the total passengers. The 'Roslyn Castle' had sailed from Falmouth with 200 passengers 'mainly from St Allen, Perranzabuloe and Camborne areas' in West Cornwall, recorded the *West Briton*.

8. Philip Payton, *Pictorial History of Australia's Little Cornwall*, Adelaide, 1978; Philip Payton, *The Cornish Miner in Australia*, Redruth,1984.

9. Ann Giffard's book *Towards Quebec,* London, 1981, which edits and comments on the diaries of two Devon families who sailed from Bideford to Quebec, one in 1848 and one in 1855, suggests that crossings from small Westcountry ports were often 'unsensational', carrying migrants 'in conditions no worse than those which they were accustomed ashore'. The two diaries suggest that the crossing was not traumatic because emigrants were with many people known to them, and the captains and crew were local people who treated the emigrants well. The emigrants also used their special skills to help the crew maintain and run the ship.

10. For example, how closely does the Cornish emigrant experience fit into the classical 'Frontier Thesis' models?

'FACE THE MUSIC!' - CHURCH AND CHAPEL BANDS IN CORNWALL

Harry Woodhouse

It is indeed a truly gratifying and encouraging circumstance to observe the happy effect of the choral service in this church. For years the people have been exhorted and entreated to attend Divine worship regularly, to be in their places in proper time, and to join in, and love the social part of the services - but in vain. Empty benches in Church and hostile contempt of her ordinances without her pale, seemed the result of ministerial efforts - for such singing as occasionally filled the aisles, there was little or no preparation - and therefore it produced irreverence rather than zeal. While the Western gallery with many disorderly occupants, monopolized altogether the privilege of praising the most high, the congregation remained uninterested and unedified auditors.

(Press report on the re-opening of Sheviock church, July 1850, with a proper choir in the chancel.)

INTRODUCTION

We are all so used to having organs in our churches and chapels, that it comes as something of a surprise to learn that for a period of about 200 years, organs were quite rare, and the singing was often accompanied by local amateur musicians. These are mentioned in all books about the history of church music,[1] and in 1948 Canon Macdermott wrote a book specifically about church bands.[2] However, he lived in East Anglia and almost all his research related to that part of Britain. Very little research seems to have been done in Cornwall. Before the Commonwealth, most large churches possessed organs, although many of them were on a much smaller scale than the instruments we have today. However, Oliver Cromwell's Order in Council of 1644 demanded the 'speedy demolishing of all organs'. The only ones which were spared were those which were in places of learning or those which could be moved into private hands. It is a common misconception that the Puritans hated music; this is not so. It is just that they

46

felt that organs were inappropriate in church. Indeed, Oliver Cromwell had an organ in his home, and employed forty-eight musicians for the wedding of one of his daughters.

On the Restoration of the Monarchy in 1660, large churches and cathedrals rapidly installed organs, but small village churches could not afford them, and in any case there was probably no-one in the village who was able to play a keyboard instrument. In many small churches singers sang the metrical psalms unaccompanied, often just using a pitch pipe to establish the pitch. Then sometimes a bass instrument, such as a 'cello, bassoon or serpent, would be used to support the bass line. By the end of the eighteenth century, many churches up and down the country possessed a band, consisting of three to eight players, playing the same parts as were used by the singers. Galleries were often provided for them, usually at the west end of the church. During the singing the congregation turned their backs to the altar and literally 'faced the music'.

The standard of musicianship, and indeed the standard of behaviour, often left much to be desired, as illustrated in many contemporary accounts. At Exeter in the 1860s, the musicians used to throw orange peel and nuts from the gallery on to the congregation below. This led to the closing of the minstrel's gallery. Sometimes things reached a stage where the vicar lost control of the service.[3] Most church bands were swept away in a surge of reforming zeal in the mid-nineteenth century, although in 1900 there were still 18 parishes in Cornwall using orchestral instruments.[4] Church galleries were taken down often without leaving a trace. The music was also reformed and the publication in 1861 of *Hymns Ancient and Modern* rendered obsolete all the manuscript books painstakingly written out by the church bands. The harmonium (or seraphine) was usually the instrument which displaced the band, although there were a few instances of other instruments being used, as at Lewannick where they had a 'cello with the organ. Where no keyboard player was available, the barrel organ was a popular choice, since little skill was required to turn the handle (except to ensure that popular ballads, often pinned on the same barrel, were not played by accident during the service). These barrel organs were often converted to 'finger organs' by the addition of a keyboard and extra pipes, or else a modern-style organ was installed. A similar pattern was to be found in non-conformist churches. When John Wesley was alive, only three chapels in England possessed organs.[5]

Given this historical background, it would seem simple for the modern researcher to collect together the history of Cornish church and chapel bands, but sadly this is not so. Cornish architects were very thorough with their removal of church galleries. The galleries were usually suspended on wooden pillars at the west end and were more or less self-supporting. Occasionally, as at Lezant, holes were made in the granite pillars, and were neatly plugged with stone after the removal of the gallery. A few church band instruments survive in museums, for example in Truro, the Isles of Scilly, Launceston and Carharrack. Some still exist in private hands. However, most seem to have disappeared without trace. Only a tiny fraction of the music has survived.

A few Cornish hymn books are known and less than a dozen manuscript books have been found so far. *Hymns Ancient and Modern* rendered them all obsolete and no doubt most finished up on the fire. The researcher is thus forced to fall back on church records. There are many history books on Cornish parishes and regions, available in libraries and bookshops, and there are excellent collections of church guides and pamphlets in the Cornish Studies Library at Redruth and in the Courteney Library at the Royal Cornwall Museum in Truro. Unfortunately, few writers of church guides seem to have had any interest in music, but sometimes several guides have been written for the same church, and (as at St Austell) occasionally one edition does contain some musical history.

Most clues are to be found in church account books, now deposited in the Cornwall Record Office, Truro. Many books are missing, but those that remain often give positive proof of the existence of a band. It is an exciting experience for the researcher to read through dozens of pages of mundane church accounts and suddenly come across 'String for the Base Viol, 2s. 5d. The present author and colleagues have studied 172 sets of church accounts in this way, and compiled over 200 pages of notes. Many other types of church record exist, but they are rarely of any musical interest, except an occasional 'Faculty' - permission from the bishop to erect a gallery. Chapel records are also preserved at the Cornwall Record Office, but they are far less complete, since it has not been compulsory for non-conformists to deposit their materials in County archives, and sadly many Cornish chapels have closed down. There are also some restrictions placed on public inspection of some chapel records. Finally, there is even now a lingering oral tradition - people are still around who remember their grandfathers playing in church or chapel bands.

INSTRUMENTS IN CORNISH CHURCHES AND CHAPELS

Canon Macdermott listed the instruments which he found had been played in church bands - but, as noted earlier, his research was concentrated in East Anglia. His list includes some unlikely candidates! It is arranged in decreasing order of frequency: violin, flute, clarinet, violoncello ('bass-viol'), bassoon, trombone, oboe, cornet, serpent, double-bass, ophicleide, cornopean, fife, baritone, cross-blown flageolet, flutina, concertina, banjo, bass-horn, French horn, keyed bugel, vamp-horn, triangle. Of these, only 14 have been recorded in Cornwall so far. Most were bought new or second-hand from music dealers, but some were home-made, like the serpent and seraphine at Breage.

The first instrument encountered in Cornish records is often a 'pitch-pipe', usually in the early eighteenth century. It consisted of a simple whistle with a plunger at the bottom to set the pitch - rather like the modern 'Swanee Whistle', or a small stopped organ pipe. There are numerous anecdotes of musical disasters, when individuals had accidentally knocked the plungers right in, setting the singers far too high. Mention of a 'flute' in the records always refers to the transverse or 'German' flute - the recorder or 'flute-à-bec' has never been found in a church. Before 1850, the flute was made of turned boxwood, with ivory rings to strengthen the joints, and only one brass key at the bottom for D sharp. Later, more keys were added, until by 1850 the flute was often made of metal, although it is still referred to as a 'woodwind' instrument. The boxwood variety tended to warp with age and go out of tune, a failing which it shared with the clarinet, oboe and bassoon. Even modern professional musicians have great difficulty keeping such an ensemble in tune, especially in a cold damp church with long intervals between the music! The 'fife' referred to in Cornish records is the familiar small flute of simple construction used in military bands. Even today, they are often to be found in Cornish antique shops.

The clarinet was similar to its modern counterpart, but made, like the flute, of boxwood with ivory rings. It had upwards of five brass keys, but the fingering was not standardised, and the author's example of this instrument cannot play F natural. The clarinet was played with a single cane reed, tied to a wooden mouthpiece, usually of ebony. It is a characteristic of the physics of clarinet design, that when it 'squeaks', it produces a horrible noise, not musically related to the note intended. It seems that this sound was often heard in Cornish churches. Indeed, the clarinettist at St Mawgan-in-Pydar used to stamp down from the gallery, go outside and dip his reed in the stream that flows past the churchyard gate.[6] The violoncello was identical to the modern instrument, but was usually referred to as the 'bass viol'. This latter instrument did exist, but the whole family of viols, with the exception of the modern double-bass, is now obsolete. The name seems to have lingered on, often in hilarious spellings. In Cornwall we have found 'Base vile', 'Beais Veial', 'Buse viol', 'Baze vial' and many others. No doubt, 'Base vile' accurately expressed the feelings of the church clerk who thus described it in the accounts. The bassoon is a bass version of the oboe, played with a double reed of cane. It has a long wooden body, doubled back on itself, and held at the side of the player. Early versions had few keys, but the number of keys increased over the years, making it easier to play difficult music. When properly played, it produces a beautiful soft buzzing sound, and was admirably suited to supporting the singers' bass line. At least it does not squeak like the clarinet. The oboe is similar in size to the clarinet, but has a slim conical bore and is played with a small double reed of cane. It started life as a very raucous shawm played outdoors by the town waites, but was tamed by giving it a smaller reed, narrower bore and placing the reed between the lips instead of uncontrolled inside the mouth. In 1800 it had only one bass key like early flutes, but the number of keys increased, as with the flute, clarinet and bassoon. The oboe does not have as great a range as the clarinet, and produces a more prominent sound.

The cornet (not to be confused with the medieval cornett) is the same as the modern brass-band instrument - not unlike the orchestral trumpet. The serpent is now quite obsolete, although modern fibreglass replicas are still made (one is played by Roger Smith in his weekly concerts in St Mary's, Isles of Scilly). It consisted of an S-shaped wooden tube, carved out of many separate pieces, glued together, and bound with black leather. It had six finger-holes, often ivory-mounted, and a variable number of (totally ineffective) brass keys. It was played with an ivory mouthpiece like a modern tuba, and thus bridges the gap between the woodwind and brass families of instruments. It is fashionable today to make fun of the serpent, but played well, it has a beautiful soft woody sound, not unlike a bass clarinet. Playing the serpent is one of the author's doubtful accomplishments. It was invented in France, probably in

A Serpent, Scilly Museum

1590 and designed initially as a church instrument - hence the name 'serpent d'eglise'. It rapidly spread to England, where it also became a military instrument. In about 1790 L.A. Frichot invented a metal upright serpent which he called the bass-horn. It was usually made of copper, and consisted of two tubes at an acute angle to each other, one carrying a long swan-necked crook, and the other a widely-flared bell. Three or four keys were usually fitted. It was a much more convenient shape to play than the serpent, and was said to have a more powerful tone. In 1821 a Frenchman, Halary, invented a brass serpent with many large brass keys, which he call the ophicleide. Elderly readers may recall it on the front cover of *Punch*. The fingering is difficult and totally illogical, but in theory at least, it is easier to play in tune than the serpent, because the vent-holes are in the right places and of adequate size. It was intended by Mendelssohn for use in his overture 'Midsummer Night's Dream'. The keyed-bugle was a British invention, and although it looks like a bugle, it has keys which open vent-holes in the side, and is thus a smaller version of the ophicleide.

Little need be said of the violin and double-bass which were the same as their modern counterparts. The violin or 'fiddle' was, however, associated in some vicars' minds with dancing and the devil, and was not welcomed in their churches.

The harmonium is a keyboard instrument which uses air pressure to sound banks of free brass reeds ('free' in the sense that they are not attached to pipes, as in a church organ oboe stop). It is fitted with an expression device which enables the player to exercise great control over the volume of sound - rather like a woodwind player and his breath control. Developed in France, it was used by Rossini in his 'Petite Messe Solenelle'. There is still an example in the remote church of St Enodoc, but harmoniums are confused in the public mind with American organs, which produce their sound by suction, not pressure, and give a more mellow sound. Tregaminion church has a fine example of the latter, complete with dummy organ pipes. The seraphine, invented in England in 1826, was a precursor of the harmonium, but achieved only limited success. Groves' *Dictionary of Music and Musicians* says it had a harsh and rasping tone, and never found favour with sensitive musicians. Perhaps the musicians of Sheviock were an exception - the instrument may still be seen there.

Church galleries have already been described, but very few survive in Cornwall. Excellent examples are to be seen in Dorset, for example in Puddletown, and at Minstead, Hampshire (where there is also a tombstone of a serpent-player, with a beautiful carving of the serpent.). A rather fanciful picture of a Cornish gallery may be seen in St Breward church. It is of 'Dr Syntax preaching' by Thomas Rowlandson (1756-1827). There are many excellent portrayals of galleries outside Cornwall, for example the superb painting 'The Village Choir' by Thomas Webster R.A. in the Victoria and Albert Museum, London. We have found references to gallery curtains in St Eval (1802), Linkinhorne (1827), Poundstock (1798), South Hill (1800), Stratton (1822),

Botus Fleming (1810), St Stephens by Saltash (1804) and St Tudy (1820, also with 'a gilted knob for the gallery'). One wonders what mischief took place during the sermons while the gallery curtains were drawn.

The following churches in Cornwall had galleries, but so far no evidence of their bands has been found: Blisland (1781), Falmouth (1686-1749), Flushing (1842), Fowey (1876), Lansallos (1871), Mylor, Pelynt (1728), Quethiock, St Breward (early 19th century), St Day (removed 1929), St Eval (repaired 1853), St Merthiana (Boscastle) (removed 1870), Tintagel (1850), Truro (St George) (replaced 1893), Veryan (1822) and Launceston (1718-1910). They are referred to in accounts and church histories as 'singing-galleries' or simply 'galleries'.

The gallery in Tregaminion Church, near Polkerris

The evidence found so far for church and chapel bands in Cornwall now follows. To avoid references of excessive length, the type of source only is given. The many shortcomings of this research must be borne in mind. An entry in the church accounts of '1824: reeds for the bassoon, 5*s*. 3*d*.' is certain evidence that there was a bassoon in the church band in 1824. The instrument may or may not have belonged to the church. However, a sparcity or lack of entries may mean several things, for example:

(a) the entry in the accounts is not specific enough - it may just say 'To Mr Jones' bill 5*s*. 3*d*'. In some cases we may know that Mr Jones was a local musical instrument dealer but this is very rare.

(b) the accounts may be missing, lost or destroyed.

(c) the instruments may have been privately owned, and the player sufficiently well-to-do to provide his own reeds/strings/ repairs.

Tregajorran Chapel band and choir in the 1860s,
Caharrack Methodist Museum

A CORNISH INSTRUMENT LIST

The source for the entries below is Cornwall Record Office, church accounts, DDP series, unless otherwise stated. References in local history books and church pamphlets are usually vague, with no source quoted. It is quite clear that the listing below must represent a tiny fraction of the total number of instruments once used in Cornwall.

ALTARNUN Clarinet 1848; strings 1856-58; harmonium 1894 West gallery removed 1865
ALTARNUN METHODIST CHAPEL Violin, cello, c.1900[7]
ANTONY Pitchpipe 1785-1792. Violin 1801-28; bassoon 1801-10; bass viol 1804-28 (replaced in 1822).

BALDHU Reputed to have had a band[8]
BALDHU CHAPEL 2 cornets and trombone c.1900. The first cornet player was killed in Wheal Jane in 1910[9]
BOCONNOC Bass viol 1822-45
BOTUS FLEMING Bass viol 1793-1838
BOYTON Bass viol 1808-65, clarinet 1808-34, flute 1813, violin 1814-25
BRADDOCK Bass viol 1823-47, flute 1808, clarinet 1825
BREAGE Mr Dobb made a serpent and seraphine for the church in 1860. Tune book of Mr Trethewey still exists[10]
BUDE HAVEN (ST MICHAEL & ALL ANGELS) Built 1835, had gallery, bass viol, flute, violin. Organ installed 1892[11]

CAMBORNE Bassoon, bass viol, flute, violin, clarinet, c.1850, Gallery removed 1862.[12] Barrel organ[13]
CARLEEN CHAPEL Locally made barrel organ 1834[14]
CARNON DOWNS CHAPEL Bassoon and other wind instruments 1837, harmonium 1896, organ 1928. Chapel lit by 80 candles in 1837[15]
CHARLESTOWN CHAPEL Bass viol 1841, seraphine 1849[16]
COLAN Bass viol 1833-43, clarinet 1835-42
CONSTANTINE Ophicleide and flute. Organ 1890. Funeral hymn[17]
CRANTOCK Bassoon 1790-1847 (new bassoon 1841, £2 2s. 0d.) clarinet 1817-49, (new clarinet 1827 & 1838), bass viol 1817-54, flute 1817-43 (new flute 1830, £1 2s. 6d.)
CREED Clarinet 1785-1808, bassoon 1786-1807, oboe 1789-1808, violin 1805
CROSSWYN (ST EWE) CHAPEL Wind and strings c.1815[18]

DAVIDSTOWE Violin 1850-69, bass viol 1850-69, organ 1877
DULOE 2 flutes 1804-06, bass viol 1805-09, harmonium and gallery removed 1860[19]

EGLOSKERRY Pitch pipe 1775 and 1791, bass viol 1804-56, violin 1820-55, harmonium 1871

FEOCK Violin 1836-44, bass viol 1836-43, keyed bugle 1836, old bassoon sold 1839 for 5s. 0d. It is said that this church had a band of 7 bassoons[20]
FEOCK, GOONPIPER CHAPEL Built 1867, gallery removed 1890. Said to have had an orchestra.[21]
FORRABURY (BOSCASTLE) Bass viol 1785-1858, bassoon 1821, 3 flutes 1823, organ 1871[22]

GARRAS METHODIST CHAPEL Clarinet 1850[23]
GRACCA CHAPEL (BUGLE) Serpent 1840[24]
GULVAL Clarinet 1824, barrel organ then finger organ 1847[25]

HAYLE (ST ELWIN) Musicians' gallery[26]

HELLAND Oboe 1802, bassoon 1806-34 (when it was exchanged for a bass viol), clarinet 1828, bass viol 1834-46

HELLESVEAR Cornet, clarinet, ophicleide, 1874[27]

ILLOGAN Bassoon and west gallery 1797-1822, organ 1864

JACOBSTOWE Pitch pipe 1774, violin 1827-65, bass viol 1827-65, harmonium 1903, organ 1919

KENWYN Pitch pipe 1787 and 1797, reeds 1822, bass viol 1823-25, barrel organ 1824 (but still a 'cello in 1825). Village orchestra had bass viol, clarinets, bassoon 1820. There is a picture of 'the village orchestra' showing clarinet, serpent, flute, double bass, violin, bassoon (no date)[28]

LADOCK 'Cello 1847-62, organ 1888

LANDULPH Bass viol 1825-48, violin 1825-47, harmonium 1859

LANEAST Possible serpent 1799, Writing not clear

LANIVET Clarinet, bass viol early 19th century, organ 1871[29]

LANLIVERY Flute 1857, 'cello 1863, harmonium 1871

LANREATH Pitch pipe 1796 and 1812, bass viol 1806-47, violin 1808-47,clarinet 1825-31, flute 1825, gallery 1834

LANTEGLOS-BY-FOWEY Bass viol 1848-58, harmonium 1884

LAUNCESTON METHODIST CHAPEL 'Instrumentalists' 1829[30]

LAWHITTON Bass viol 1812-21, organ 1888

LELANT 'band' 1737, gallery 1751, pitch pipe 1760, organ 1908

LESNEWTH Pitch pipe 1812-16, harmonium 1877

LEWANNICK Pitch pipe 1776-89, bass viol 1807-40, violin 1811, organ 1832 (with bass viol), harmonium 1872

LEZANT 'Minstrels, choir and singing loft'[31]

LINKINHORNE Bass viol 1801-28, violin 1817-23

LISKEARD (ST MARTINS) Gallery 1824-32, violin 1826-28, bass viol 1826-28, organ 1844 (7) 'violins, 'cellos, flutes, clarinets, bassoons and scorpions, to make sweet music for the good people of Liskeard'[32]

LISKEARD (GREENBANK CHAPEL) '2 cornets, 3 flutes, 2 violins, double bass'[33]

LITTLE PETHERICK Bass viol 1818-58, 2 flutes 1858[34]

LOOE (EAST) Flute 1811, harmonium 1873[35]

LUDGVAN Gallery 1798-1833, bass viol 1824-56, violin 1837-56, clarinet 1839-53, bass horn 1856, organ 1860 [36]

LUXULYAN Gallery 1806, pitch pipe 1806, clarinet 1815-43, bassoon 1816, bass viol 1822-23, flute 1832, harmonium 1870

MABE CHAPEL (TRENOWETH) Ophicleide, 2 fifes c.1880[37]

MADRON 'orchestra' 1750, bass viol 1806-38, 2 clarinets 1808-27, violins 1813-14, gallery 1836, flute 1827 'organ' 1840, barrel organ until 1859[38]

MAKER Before 1874 had gallery, flute, pitch pipe, then harmonium, then organ 1875

MARAZION (MARKET JEW) Bass viol 1805-14, gallery 1841

MAWNAN Gallery 1803-25, 'bass reeds' 1828, clarinet 1832, organ 1906

MENHENIOT Pitch pipe 1793, organ 1804

MEVAGISSEY Flute 1845, strings no date, harmonium 1855. Poem describes clarinet, flute, oboe, cello, violins[40]

MORWENSTOWE Bass viol 1813-63, violin 1813-63, gallery 1848, harmonium, organ[41]

MOUSEHOLE Violin, bass viol, flute c1860[42]

NEWLYN EAST Gallery 1823, clarinet 1835, strings 1835, harmonium 1868[43]

NEWQUAY (CHURCH OF ST MICHAEL) Flute 1858, organ 1881[44]
NEWQUAY (WESLEYAN CHAPEL) Cello 1852[45]
NORTH HILL Strings 1829-40, gallery 1847, organ 1908
NORTH PETHERWIN Gallery 1813, bass viol 1851
NORTH TAMERTON Pitch pipes 1783, bass viol 1794-1884, flutes 1884, harmonium 1887, organ 1891

OTTERHAM (CAMELFORD) Gallery 1823, strings 1823

PADSTOW Gallery 1817, bass viol 1818-52, flute 1834
PENRYN CHAPEL Bass viol, 1 or 2 flutes, serpent prior to organ 1859, harmonium 1888[46]
PENZANCE 'ORGAN CHURCH' WESLEYAN Band walked out when organ was installed[47]
PERRANUTHNOE Bass viol 1818-33, clarinet 1831-34, organ 1884
PHILLACK Bass viol 1804-34, clarinet 1809-30, violin 1819
PORT ISAAC CHAPEL Harmonium with violin *c*1900, organ 1920[48]
POUGHILL (ST OLAF'S) Gallery 1779-1860, pitch pipe 1780, flute 1806-19, bass viol 1787-1855, violin 1807-27, harmonium 1875, organ 1882
POUNDSTOCK (ST NEOT'S) Gallery 1798-1891, pitch pipe 1783, bassoon 1789, bass viol 1790-1849, violin 1798-1860, oboe 1800-01
PROBUS Gallery 1851, 'automatic reed organ' *c*1850 [49]

REDRUTH (ST EUNY'S) Gallery removed 1878, 'orchestra' before that, harmonium 1873, barrel organ, organ[50]
RILLA MILL CHAPEL Serpent, bassoon[51]

ST AUSTELL Gallery 1829, flutes 1831, barrel organ 1820, seraphine 1854, organ 1872[52]
ST BLAZEY Gallery 1826-97, bassoon 1800-06, oboe 1800-04
ST BURYAN Gallery 1851, clarinet 1817, violin 1826, bass viol 1827, harmonium 1880
ST CLEMENT Clarinet 1806, bass viol 1827, violin 1827[53]
ST DOMINIC Strings 1800-09, bass viol 1808
ST ERME Bassoon 1819
ST ERVAN Bass viol, now at Little Petherick[54]
ST GENNYS Pitch pipe 1802, violin 1802-55, oboe 1802-07, bass viol 1819-55[55]
ST IVES Gallery 1639-1840, bass viol, clarinet (24), barrel organ 1831[56]
ST KEVERNE Bassoon 1822-24, 2 clarinets 1822[57]
ST MARTIN BY LOOE Flutes 1819-47, violins 1819-54, bass viol 1819-54, gallery removed and organ installed 1878[58]
ST MARY'S, ISLES OF SCILLY (OLD CHAPEL)[59] 2 clarinets 1837, 2 violins, bass viol, serpent
ST MAWGAN IN PYDAR 2 flutes, 2 clarinets, 1 or 2 bass viols until gallery removed in 1860, then harmonium[60]
ST MELLION Bass viol 1841-49, organ 1893
ST MICHAEL PENKIVEL Pitch pipe 778, clarinet 1802-20, bass viol 1838-65, organ 1907
ST MINVER Bass viol 1836, violin 1841
ST NEOT Bass viol 1799-1839, oboe 1799-1803, flute 1804-29 clarinet 1805, violin 1813-23, gallery 1819
ST PINNOCK (NEAR LISKEARD) Bass viol 1815-24, 'small orchestra' assembled in 1903 for coronation[61]
ST PIRAN (PERRANZABULOE) Gallery and string band before 1873[62]
ST SAMPSONS Clarinet 1845, bass viol 1845-60, flute 1853, harmonium 1876
ST STEPHENS (SALTASH) Gallery 1788, bass viol 1789-46, violins 1823-46[63]
ST TUDY Gallery 1741, pitch pipe 1768 and 1798, 'musical instruments' 1809, bass viol 1812-22, clarinet 1817-19, bassoon 1821
ST WENN Oboe 1789, pitch pipe 1809, clarinet 1810-34, bass viol 1820-38, bassoon 1835
ST WINNOW Bassoon 1805-25, 2 flutes 1807-26, bass viol 1813-27, clarinet 1814-26
SENNEN Had a band[64]

SHEVIOCK Gallery 1741, pitch pipe 1768 and 1790, bass viol 1814-42, 2 violins 1820-42, seraphine 1842 (actually an Aeolophon)

SITHNEY 'Musical instruments' 1828, bassoon 1836-39, bass viol 1837-38, harmonium 1873

SOUTH HILL Gallery 1777, bass viols 1798-1827, violin 1800-24, organ 1881

STICKER CHAPEL Bass viol 1847-56, flute 1856, harmonium 1856[65]

STRATTON Oboe 1788-95, violin 1789, bass viol 1795-1845, gallery 1811, organ 1847

TALLAND Pitch pipe 1778, bassoon 1790, strings 1809, bass viol 1819-55, flute 1820-38[66]

TORPOINT Bass viol 1808-19, flute 1819, gallery 1819[67]

TREGAJORRAN CHAPEL Serpent, ophicleide, flute *c.*1860[68]

TREGONEY (ST CUBY'S) Gallery 1826, flute 1827 (? writing poor), organ 1831[69]

TREGREHAN MILLS CHAPEL (ST AUSTELL) Flute before harmonium 1880[70]

TRENEGLOS (BUDE) Bass viol 1805-32, gallery 1805, violins 1831

TRESMEER Bass viol 1806-14, oboe 1806-14, violin 1806-14

TREWEN Pitch pipe 1797, bass viol 1802

TYWARDREATH Oboe 1785, bassoon 1812, flutes 1815-49, bass viol 1815-27, gallery 1819

WEEK STMARY Bass viol 1818-62[71]

WHITSTONE Violins, bass viol, flute 1864

ZENNOR Gallery 1722, bass viol 1830, clarinet 1833 , also flute, violin before 1890

From the above Instrument Frequency list of 124 churches and chapels listed
the following frequency table has been compiled:

Instrument	Number of Locations Recorded	Earliest Date Found	Latest Date Found	Mean Date Found
Bass viol / cello	79	1785	1884	1834
Violin	41	1789	1900	1844
Flute	41	1804	1884	1844
Clarinet	36	1785	1874	1829
Bassoon	23	1786	1847	1816
(Pitch pipe)	20	1760	1812	1786
Oboe	11	1785	1808	1796
Serpent	8	1799	1860	1829
Ophicleide	4	1860	1880	1870
Double Bass	3	-	-	-
Cornet	3	1874	1900	1887
Bass horn	1	1856	1856	1856
Fife	1	1880	1880	1880
Trombone	1	1900	1900	1900
Keyed Bugle	1	1836	1836	1836
Harmonium/ seraphine	31	1842	1903	1872
Barrel organ	8	1820	1859	1839

The frequency of mention of the instruments follows roughly that found by Canon Macdermott in East Anglia, except that Cornwall seems to have had far more bass viols. Band sizes in the locations studied varied from a single player to six players (Kenwyn and St Mary's, Isles of Scilly), with many churches and chapels having four or five players, usually mixed string and wind. Again this seems to follow the pattern in the rest of Britain. It seems highly probable that most Cornish parish churches and chapels had an instrumentalist or band at some time during their history. It is also worth noting that Cornwall is, as a result of the research presented here, probably the first region in Britain to have been studied in a systematic fashion. Canon Macdermott collected musical anecdotes all his life, but it is unlikely that he ever systematically searched church records in East Anglia.

CONCLUSION

Our Cornish research has studied every church account book in the Cornwall Record Office, from about 1750 to 1910. Experience showed that searching outside these dates was non-productive. Every church pamphlet in the Cornish Studies Library (Redruth) and the Courteney Library at the Royal Cornwall Museum was studied, as well as a great many found *in situ* in churches. Every accessible Cornish history book was studied for references to church bands (a great many of these contain amusing anecdotes, but no sources or dates - for example, the works of Sir Arthur Quiller Couch and A.K.Hamilton Jenkin). This was supplemented by the recollections of people who had heard the author's lectures/recitals, or had heard his broadcasts on *BBC Radio Cornwall*. However, the research has not been so exhaustive with regard to non-conformist chapels. Further work could usefully be done, particularly in the identification of hitherto 'lost' chapel records.

ACKNOWLEDGEMENTS

The author would like to express his grateful thanks to Dr Richard McGrady, the staffs of the libraries at the Cornwall Record Office, the Royal Institution of Cornwall, the Cornish Studies Library, and his wife and friends, John and Caroline Black.

This work was carried out with the assistance of a Caroline L. Kemp Research Scholarship, awarded by the University of Exeter.

REFERENCES

1. Nicholas Temperley, *The Music of the English Parish Church*, Cambridge, 1983; Kenneth R. Long, *The Music of the English Church*, London, 1972; Christopher Dearnley, *English Church Music 1650-1750*, London 1970; Friedrick Blume, *Protestant Church Music*, New York, 1974.
2. K. H. Macdermott, *The Old Church Gallery Minstrels*, London, 1948.
3. Macdermott, 1948, p. 7.

4. H. Miles Brown, *Truro Diocesan News Leaflet*, September 1953.
5. Blume, 1974.
6. Charles Lee, *Portrait of a Cornish Musician, from the City*, n.d.
7. Trewynt Methodist Museum.
8. Macdermott, 1948, p. 67.
9. Private communication to the author.
10. Private communication to the author.
11. *Budehaven (St Michael & All Angels) Church Guide*
12. Charles Thomas, *Christian Antiquities of Camborne*, Truro, 1967.
13. Macdermott, 1948, p. 67.
14. Thomas Shaw, *A History of Church Methodism*, Truro, 1967.
15. *Carnon Downs Chapel Guide*
16. Cornwall Record Office, chapel records, MR series.
17. *Constantine Church Guide*
18. J. Kitto Roberts, *The Mevagissy Independents 1625-1946*, Taunton, 1946.
19. H. Miles Brown, *The Catholick Revival in Cornish Anglicanism*, n.d.
20. Macdermott, 1948, p. 25.
21. *Feock, Goonpiper Chapel Guide*
22. *Forrabury (Bocastle) Church Guide*
23. *Garras Methodist Chapel*
24. Private communication to the author.
25. *Gulval Church Guide*
26. *Hayle (St Elwin) Church Guide*
27. Shaw, 1967.
28. *Kenwyn Church Guide*
29. Private communication to the author.
30. Shaw, 1967, p. 46
31. *Lezant Church Guide*
32. *Liskeard (St Martin's) Church Guide*
33. Paul Bolitho, *The Story of Methodism in the Liskeard Circuit 1751-1967*, Liskeard, 1967.
34. Private communication to the author.
35. *Looe (East) Church Guide*
36. *Ludgvan Church Guide*
37. Private communication to the author
38. *Madron Church Guide*
39. *Maker Church Guide*
40. Roberts, 1946
41. *Morwenstowe Church Guide*
42. Shaw, 1967
43. S. Teague Husband, *Old Newquay*, Newquay, 1923.
44. Husband, 1923/1984.
45. Husband, 1923/1984.
46. R. J. Roddis, *Penryn*, Truro, 1964.
47. Private communication to the author
48. Monica Winstanley, *High Tide at Padstow*, Padstow, 1978.
49. Macdermott, 1948, p. 42.
50. *Redruth (St Euny's) Church Guide*
51. Private communication to the author.
52. Richard McGrady, *Music and Musicians in Early 19th-century Cornwall*, Exeter, 1991.
53. *St Clement Church Guide*
54. *St Ervan Church Guide*
55. Roger Parnall, *Wreckers and Wrestlers*, Truro, 1973.
56. Macdermott, 1948, p. 73.
57. *St Keverne Church Guide*
58. *St Martin by Looe Church Guide*
59. Local Museum.

60. *St Mawgan in Pydar Church Guide*
61. *St Pinnock Church Guide*
62. *St Piran (Perranzabuloe) Church Guide*
63. *St Stephens (Saltash) Church Guide*
64. Macdermott, 1948, p. 5.
65. Cornwall Record Office, chapel records, MR series.
66. *Talland Church Guide*
67. H. Miles Brown, *What to look for in Cornish Churches*, Newton Abbot, 1973.
68. Private communication to the author.
69. *Tregoney (St Cuby's) Church Guide*
70. *Tregrehan Mills Church Guide*
71. *Week St Mary Church Guide*
72. P. A. S. Pool, *A Cornish Farmer's Diary*, Hayle, 1977.

RE-INVENTING CORNWALL:
CULTURE CHANGE ON THE EUROPEAN
PERIPHERY
Bernard Deacon and Philip Payton

MAPS OF CORNISH MEANING

Several years ago, a contributor to a conference on Cornish culture made a plea from the heart, 'Why can't we,' she asked, 'just find out what it is?' A simple question perhaps, but the answer was not so simple, partly because no-one present could agree on what the word 'culture' meant. Some restrict it to mean fine art, Shakespearian plays or historical buildings, elements that can 'be skilfully packaged and sold as heritage'.[1] On such a definition, the Newlyn and StIves schools of painters become examples of 'Cornish culture'. For others, culture means those artefacts that give different societies their particular style, whether it be stone axes, engine houses or Cornish pasties. Identifying 'Cornish culture' then becomes a task of listing definably 'Cornish' artefacts, a list that often runs dry fairly quickly after the pasty and the saffron bun, requiring early recourse to recently 'invented' symbols such as the 'Cornish Kilt' and the 'Cornish National Tartan'. On the other hand some do not bother to define Cornish culture at all. It is just something that requires 'defending', 'protecting' or 'saving', or even 'promoting' or 'enhancing'. Yet others will take culture to mean a way of life, a set of relationships between people; their customs, their dialects, their sports, their politics, their socio-economic activities, and - ultimately - the way in which they see themselves, the quality of 'feeling Cornish', of belonging to an imagined Cornish community.

This last comes closest to the definition of culture used here. But it is not the whole story. Customs, ways of speech, sporting activities are symbols that have a particular meaning for people. These symbols can only be understood through their meaning and that meaning, in turn, is historically constructed within a discrete culture. The culture of a particular social group can be viewed as its 'meanings system', the way it makes sense of certain symbols. The stone axes, the engine houses, the pasties are interpreted by a map of meanings. They can be seen as having a particular cultural resonance within Cornish culture but they will have other meanings or no meaning at all when viewed from other cultures. Moreover, the map of meanings has a further function. It allows people to interpret the changing social reality around them. It gives them a set of ideas for making sense of and coping with that changing reality. Different cultures will cope in different ways. Furthermore, the map of meanings marks out the distinctiveness of their own locality.[2] Cornish culture, therefore, is that meanings system adopted by the group of people who define themselves as 'Cornish'. From this perspective, culture must be viewed as a dynamic process, subject to constant change and re-negotiation and contested by other cultures with their own maps of meaning. Indeed, within this context it is no co-incidence that rapid socio-economic change since 1945 (in particular, massive in-migration from across the Tamar) has led not to the demise of Cornish culture that some had predicted, but rather to its re-definition and re-assertion.

In Britain, cultural studies became a booming academic industry during the 1980s. However, in Cornwall there has been surpisingly little work on Cornish culture. The first writings on the nature of Cornish culture tended to emerge from a nationalist paradigm.[3] To such writers Cornish culture is a threatened species. Centuries of anglicisation have reduced Cornish culture to something virtually indistinguishable from English culture, yet through it all there remains a residual Cornish identity, which can be regenerated by the Celtic Revival. What this approach fails to explain is the persistence of a strong, popular sense of Cornish cultural identity. Clearly, being Cornish still has a meaning for many thousand Cornish people. The nature of the map of meanings that makes up Cornish culture and produces the Cornish identity has only recently been subjected to serious analysis, mainly by historians, but also sociologists and political scientists, who have begun to take an interest in the nature of Cornish cultural identity.[4] The time has come for a preliminary synthesis of their findings.

In this article, the nature of Cornish culture is discussed, identifying the symbols that give it meaning and assessing the consequence of this map of meaning. The roots of the modern Cornish identity are investigated, and suggestions are made as to how that identity has changed over the last hundred years or so and is still changing.[5]

AN EMERGING CULTURE : THE MINING - METHODIST SOCIETY OF THE EARLY 19TH CENTURY

Raymond Williams has suggested a three-fold model of cultures.[6] There are dominant cultures, which impose a hegemonic map of meanings on society; emergent cultures, which are in the process of being formed; and residual cultures, which are in the process of being marginalised. By the 17th and 18th centuries, the older Cornish culture, associated with a Celtic vernacular and clearly non-English meanings (after all, the Cornish rose three times in rebellion against the English state in the 40 years after 1497) was being firmly marginalised. It was overlaid by an emerging, reconstructed culture of

Cornishness based on the twin poles of mining and Methodism. This, by the early 19th century, had become the locally dominant culture, structuring the meanings Cornish people gave to 'being Cornish'. Elements of the older culture did survive (for example dialect words inherited from the Cornish language), occasionally informing or even moulding aspects of the new culture, but the culture of industrial Cornwall was fundamentally different to that which had gone before. And yet, it was still identifiably 'Cornish', and was articulated as such.

Deep mining, stimulated by the application of steam engine technology, revolutionised West Cornwall in the 18th century and brought this peripheral region on the edge of Europe into the vanguard of modernisation. By 1750 an estimated 25% of the population were dependent on copper and tin mining, and by the mid-19th century around a third of the people were directly employed in mining.[7] Meanwhile, the mining industry had expanded territorially across the length of the land to incorporate East Cornwall under its influence. Highly capitalised mining and proto-industrialisation was both a product of and, to some extent, a purveyor of universalist principles. Contemporaries, in Cornwall as in other areas, gloried in the new triumphalist culture of industrialism.[8] Davies Gilbert, for example, in the introduction to a publication of a medieval Cornish drama in 1826 could still write that 'no one more sincerely rejoices than the author of this ancient mystery that the Cornish dialect of the Celtic or Gaelic languages has ceased altogether from being used by the inhabitants of Cornwall'.[9]

With a new, or at least a restructured, industrial base came a new religion - Methodism. John Wesley visited Cornwall on 32 occasions in the years after 1743 and, by the 1780s, Methodism, with its values of self-help and thrift, its egalitarianism and democratic tendencies, had taken a firm hold on the Cornish people, especially in the rural mining areas. This emergent culture of mining-Methodism had major social consequences. Heard, in 1817, wrote that 'those local habits which might once have been deemed unconquerable, have almost completely disappeared',[10] while the impression of rapid cultural change was echoed by Thomas Quiller-Couch in 1864, 'the rapid fluctuations and changes of the last 50 years have done more to alter and change (popular customs) than many previous centuries of stagnation, or of very gradual progress.'[11]

What did this new culture involve? Its central meaning was derived from a developed self-awareness of what has been called 'industrial prowess'.[12] The Cornish were acknowledged world leaders in the field of deep metal mining. This led to a confidence that permeated both the new bourgeoisie, like Davies Gilbert, and the common people. The positive comments of visitors to Cornwall echo the self-confidence of the Cornish people. 'The inhabitants of Cornwall . . . are marked by peculiar features of character. Its men are sturdy and bold, honest and sagacious; its women lovely and modest, courteous and unaffected.' Even, this writer continued, their proverbs prove 'the results of good sense, a nice observation acting upon experience; applying to the transactions of public as well as private life'.[13] This confident, assertive identity based on industrial success, or at least a perception of industrial success, and tempered by a communal religion with a strong egalitarian strand, was grounded in homogenous, single-industry communities where commonly-held values arose out of close-knit contacts at work, in the chapel and in the community itself. Gill Burke has noted the strong communal support systems of the mid-19th century, the role of feast days and markets and the customs of informal community support and censure, such as effigy-burning or kettle bands, all of which provided security for the individual living in this culture.[14] At the same time, the newly-dominant culture of Cornishness had incorporated many pre-industrial elements. Feast days have been mentioned, but to these we can add wrestling, a rich repertoire of customs and folktales, an expressive dialect - all of which went to produce a confident identity growing out of the twin symbols of mining and Methodism.[15] It was an identity which was asserted internally within Cornwall as 'Cornish', which was recognised externally as 'Cornish' (and therefore at some level 'different' from 'English'), and which was cohesive and integrated enough to allow its re-construction in Cornish communities overseas.

CREATING THE 19TH CENTURY POPULAR CULTURE

However, this culture did not survive the 19th century unscathed. Just as one period of capital investment had helped produce the distinct Cornish culture of the mid-19th century, another phase of development deposited yet another layer of meaning on Cornishness in the fourth quarter of the 19th century. Cornwall's industrialisation had, in fact, been unbalanced and too specialised and had failed to diversify. As uneven development led to the transference of capital investment to other parts of the globe after the crash of, first, copper and then tin mining in the 1860s and 1870s, so this produced other layers of meaning to be grafted onto the basic mining-Methodist cultural identity.[16]

We can best understand the popular Cornish culture that emerged by the Edwardian period by focusing on four cultural changes that began to operate by the 1880s. The first of these was the import and influence of mass urban cultural forms based on Britain's newly-homogenous industrial working-class towns and cities. The other three were products of the local factor of economic stagnation, and were, first, the international links forged by the mass emigration of Cornish people; second, the changing form of patriarchal structures in the local culture; and third, the consequences of material poverty.

With the rise of mass literacy, better communications via the railways and popular newspapers, influences from England and Wales, and particularly industrial working-class England and Wales, were introduced into Cornwall from the 1870s onwards. In the homogenous working-class communities of the North of England, the Midlands and South Wales new male-dominated cultural forms had emerged, for example, mass spectator sports, competitive musical leisure activities, and mass politics. Some of these were enthusiastically adopted in the industrial areas of Cornwall, particularly in the west. For example, rugby football was imported into Cornwall in the early 1870s, at first by returning public schoolboys and university students. But it was soon co-opted by the working class in West Cornwall and became a popular spectator sport. Similarly, the musical talents of Cornish people, talents that in the early 19th century found their outlet almost solely in hymn singing or small church and chapel bands, were transformed and organised into brass and silver bands or male voice choirs. These, despite originating elsewhere, were to become identified by Cornish people as somehow 'Cornish', and entwined inextricably with their own regional identity. This process of co-option of other cultures' symbols continued to the present day, as the re-definition of the popular song *Little Lize* (or *Little Eyes*) in the 1950s suggests.[17] In the process, however, Cornish culture took on a more working-class appearance, particularly in the remaining industrial heartlands. This is illustrated by H.D.Lowry's novel *Wheal Darkness*, set in a semi-fictitious late 19th century Camborne, which displays unmistakable similarities with the mass urban British working-class culture of the period.[18]

This raises a problem. Should we define these phenomena as 'Cornish culture', or were they just a local variant of the emergent urban working-class culture of the late 19th century? The simple answer is that although the symbols may have come out of a general class culture, they were themselves transformed on arrival in Cornwall and co-opted into the local culture. These symbols had, within a generation, taken on meanings of Cornishness, and had painlessly merged with the previous mining-Methodist cultural symbols. In short, they had become an indistinguishable part of popular Cornish culture, enhancing and perpetuating the identity of 'industrial prowess'.

Indeed, the economic problems following the 1860s themselves added new symbols and meanings to Cornishness. During the years from 1840 to 1900 at least 180,000 Cornish people moved permanently overseas, whilst others went and returned again, especially after the early 1870s. In some parts of the globe, notably South Australia, recognisably Cornish communities arose.[19] Here, the mining-Methodist cultural identity of Cornwall persisted and was in turn overlaid by local elements. The links between Cornwall and Australia, North America and South Africa led to a briefly-significant international culture of Cornishness, an identity that grew out of the practical, economic necessity of 'networking' (a communication system that kept a mobile emigrant community abreast of news and opportunities in the new lands) but which reflected the central importance of the Cornish in developing so many international mining areas, thus further reinforcing the sense of 'industrial prowess'.[20]

Some people in Cornwall were more attuned to events at the other side of the world than they were to life in England. These overseas links were maintained and deepened by the flow of communications between Cornwall and the Cornish diaspora. Letters were augmented by newspaper reports from the New World. These were added to in turn by the financial link which may have resulted in as much as £1 million a year being sent back to Cornwall from South Africa alone in the 1900s, or enough to keep around 40,000 people in basic standards of comfort. Morover, the Cornish were well aware that their technological expertise had facilitated the expansion of these new lands, while institutional links (from Cornish Associations to international Methodist activities) served to emphasise the relationship between Cornwall and its emigrant communities abroad. Nevertheless, this international Cornish cultural identity was a short-lived phenomenon and, as the mines that gave the exiled communities their economic base were exhausted or closed down for other reasons, the communities themselves invariably fragmented and dispersed, as happened in the Moonta area of South Australia in 1923.[21]

De-industrialisation also had an effect on the structures of patriarchy in local culture. Gill Burke has suggested that women's role in the culture changed after the 1860s. Before then, the bal maidens provided a model of free, independent behaviour, and were not seen as dependent, clinging feminine inferiors, but exhibited a marked lack of deference to men. There is evidence of this in the fiction of 'authors, whose bourgeois position might have inclined them to develop a feminine model of Cornish mining womanhood, of women acting independently of their men and of women's words being listened to with respect.'[22] However, the 'independent bal maiden' was a victim of technological change together with the shrinking mining sector after the early 1870s. Within just 25 years, most of them had been phased out of the workforce and the model was no longer available to Cornish women.

Nevertheless, the picture is not necessarily one of an increasingly patriarchal culture. While the economic changes (longer hours for men, less paid work for women) located women more firmly in the domestic sphere, it did lead to their increased autonomy in the management of family affairs, particularly financial affairs, especially given that emigration resulted, after 1870, in a skewed sex structure, with this 'world without (young) men' being particularly marked in the rural, ex-mining parishes.[23] Fiction of the 1890s (for example, Henry Harris's short story 'Trial by Pasty') also indicates that the independent non-deferential Cornish woman had by no means disappeared.[24] And women must have had a strategic, though so far unexplored, role in reproducing the Cornish culture of the crucial last quarter of the 19th century. How this role interacted with the male-dominated features such as rugby football, brass and silver bands, and male-voice choirs, is an intriguing paradox that has yet to be resolved.

Yet women, more than men, experienced a declining quality of life as the informal support systems of chapel and community re-structured themselves after the 1870s. The transition of chapel control to the middle class, especially in the towns, the waning of feast days and the decline of those communal practices which served to enhance 'social solidarity', were all important qualitative changes in the culture.[25] The older communal practices lingered longest in the industrial rural areas - perhaps in the clay district of mid-Cornwall. For example, in 1903 at Bugle a divorced man and his girlfriend, whose behaviour had offended villagers, could still be buried in effigy.[26] But this was by this time an exceptional occurrence.

The last three decades of the 19th century and the first of the 20th, as well as seeing the co-opting of elements from English working class culture, the brief flowering of an international dimension and a re-definition of the role of women, also saw the general restructuring of the culture - towards dependency and 'paralysis', and away from the proud, confident assertiveness of the mid-19th century. 'The Cornwall of the early 1900s, dependent so pathetically upon the energy of her emigres in distant South Africa, was a far cry from that vibrant, self-confident, innovative land that existed only a half century or so before.'[27]

This culture of dependency had two aspects; first, a pervasive sense of loss, fatalism and even hopelessness that is well attested in the Cornish fiction of the later 1890s, notably Henry Harris's story 'Cousin Jacky', where a returning migrant finds only desolation and despair at his home village and takes the obvious option available to him and emigrates again, or the same author's 'Souls for Gold', which laments the moral effects of the rush to South Africa on the communities left behind in Cornwall.[28] The stories in H.D.Lowry's *Wreckers and Methodists* also powerfully articulate this sense of loss.[29] The second aspect was the production of a culture of poverty. Heroism in the face of grinding day to day hardship became a social virtue; a carefulness with money and a more inward looking austere attitude to life accompanied this mood. This seems like the puritan, almost Calvinist, side of early 19th century Methodism without its accompanying redeeming features of emotional intensity and mass revivals. Perhaps this is what D.H.Lawrence meant when, during the First World War, he caricatured the Cornish people as 'inertly selfish, like insects gone cold, living only for money, mean and afraid'.[30] Perhaps too, it is reflected in the attitude of the returning miner in Lawrence's short-story 'Samson and Delilah', set in St Just-in-Penwith in the First World War.[31]

MAKING-DO : CORNISH POPULAR CULTURE IN THE FIRST HALF OF THE 20TH CENTURY.

The occupational base of 19th century Cornish culture, thriving local communities dominated by a single industry, was - outside the clay district and perhaps the towns of Camborne and Falmouth - a thing of the past by the 1920s. With its occupational underpinning destroyed and replaced by a chronic level of male unemployment that peaked at 25% in 1932, and with a continuing high propensity to emigrate, Cornish popular culture fossilised. It was a defensive culture, increasingly confined to the working class, unable to construct distinct cultural values for its remaining symbols. The rise of greater occupational opportunities for the middle class and the slow emergence of a national professional labour market was excerbating this trend, by leading to a cultural division of labour. As early as 1935, a survey of 'Cornish leaders' disclosed that only 42% had been born in Cornwall (and this included various trades unionists, who were virtually all Cornish born). Furthermore, more than half of that minority born in Cornwall had been educated in England.[32] In effect, the middle class had largely moved away from the Cornish cultural identity which still permeated the working-class. The working class culture that remained became a private, rather than a public expression of Cornishness. The Cornish working class was trapped in a culture of 'making-do', which represented resignation and adaptation to the structures of social domination and an unpredictable, but generally stagnant, economy.[33] It had been a matter of pride that, in the economic crisis of 1921, 'the most disastrous year in history' according to the *West Briton*, that 'one of the striking features in the mining district has been the manner in which poor people have literally shared their crusts with each other'. In a similar vein, the mayor of Penzance reported that 'there were at Penzance children practically starving and men and women suffering in secret hunger and privation without murmuring.'[34]

In an interesting parallel there was, at the same time, a tendency by local middle-class observers to re-emphasise the individualism and independence supposedly inherent in the Cornish character.[35] But this aspect of individualism and independence seems strangely at odds with the culture of dependency of the 1900s and the tin miners' choir which was forced to travel the length and breadth of Britain in 1921/22 literally begging for alms. The Cornish people, it was argued, had a long tradition of individualism, dating back to a Celtic settlement pattern and the independent farmer-tinner of medieval Cornwall. However, to make sense of this, we must be careful to unpack the two concepts, individualism and independence. They are not necessarily identical. In 1824, at the height of the culture of industrial prowess and confidence, Hitchens and Drew had argued that the Cornish had a 'spirit of independence (which) not only pervades their general actions, but it enters into their various views, and incorporates itself with their conflicting opinions'.[36] This was an independence of opinion born of a dynamic industrial community with a relatively weak landed gentry and with probably easier access to land than the norm in England. But an independence of opinion seemed to rest quite comfortably with another 'equally conspicuous' feature - 'accustomed to associate in bodies, they mutually encourage each other to perseverance, even on occasions when all rational hopes of success have taken their leave. Hence "One and All", accompanied with three huzzas will infallibly reanimate their drooping spirits, in the midst of a doubtful exploit'.[37] What this implies is an independence of opinion allied with communal economic activities. It is a far cry from Adam Smith's rational economic individualist. By the inter-war period, paradoxically, there had been an increase in individualism (at least ideologically) but a decrease in independence since the early 19th century.

A culture of making-do, defensive, increasingly restricted to the private domain and limited to the working class, was, by the 1940s, definitely a residual culture in Raymond Williams' terms. Yet we must not underestimate its continued meaning for the majority of Cornish people. Every now and then there could be still a rekindling of the old Cornish pride. The symbolic catalyst for this proved to be rugby football. Adopted as the working-class sport of West Cornwall in the late 19th century, the Cornish rugby team disappointingly failed to make headway in the grim years of the end of the century. Indeed, it took two decades before it recorded its first victory against the arch enemy in neighbouring Devon. But in the 1900s its fortunes improved, mirroring the temporary up-turn in the Cornish economy and the false new dawn of the Edwardians' mini-boom in mining. In 1908 the team won the County Championship to sometimes almost hysterical scenes of rejoicing on the part of Cornishmen. Rugby had become a symbol of Cornishness, an outlet - almost the only one - for the collective expression of the cultural identity. Periodically afterwards - in the 1920s, the 1940s and again in 1969, rugby proved the catalyst for an outburst of Cornishness, indicating the stubborn persistence of the cultural identity.[38] In his *Up From the Lizard*, J.C.Trewin recalled the season of 1927-28 when Cornwall almost won the County Championship, and the team included the almost legendary figures of C.G.Gosling from Torpoint, Roy Jennings of Redruth, and George Jago from Penryn: 'opponents would be alarmed by the arrival of a small regiment of Cornishmen in their rosettes of black and gold: it was their habit to chant Trelawney before the game, and cheer frantically to the end'.[39]

This apparent paradox - an increasingly fossilised culture, yet a surprisingly persistent identity - is partly explained by a wider paradox. Despite, or perhaps because of its fossilisation after the 1870s, Cornish culture became in some respects even more differentiated from English cultures. The internationalisation of the culture as a result of emigration has already been noted. Another difference can be seen in terms of political culture. The weakness of trade unions and (to a lesser extent) of the Labour Party before the 1940s meant that Cornwall's political culture became distinctly different from the general British one. Conservative-Liberal party contestation remained the norm in Cornwall, while the rest of Britain was moving swiftly towards a pattern of Conservative-Labour party conflict.[40] While Cornish political culture remained firmly 'different' it was also firmly marginalised, and Cornish politicians themselves were paralysed in the face of chronic structural economic problems. The paralysis of Cornish political culture is illustrated by the depoliticisation and parochialism of Cornish local politics after the 1890s, although even this could take on new meaning by the 1980s and be viewed as a proud example of Cornwall's 'independent' tradition.

NEW DIRECTIONS, NEW MEANINGS

New ways of representing older social processes are not confined to the re-interpretation of Cornish local politics. In the late 1890s, appalled at the 'evil days on which mining and . . . agriculture have fallen' a section of the Cornish intelligentsia broke ranks with the culture of industrial prowess by supporting the extension of tourism as the only hope for rebuilding the Cornish economy.[41] While it is difficult to imagine those horny handed 'able bodied sons forced to emigrate by the thousands' turning their attentions to waiting on table, this was at least an attempt to face up to the problems of the Cornish economy. In fact, the tourist project had already gathered pace without the need for the intervention of the local literate classes. Tourists had begun to arrive in larger numbers after the 1880s, while the investment by the Great Western Railway company in seaside hotels and its vigorous advertising campaign based on the concept of the 'Cornish Riviera Express' after 1904 gave a great boost to tourism.

Urry has pointed out how tourism, by emphasising the 'difference' of a particular place in order to sell it, can add to the 'symbolic repertoire' of locality, re-emphasising and articulating existing differences.[42] This was certainly true in Cornwall's case, although, as the development of tourism was controlled largely from outside Cornwall and written about by people outside the Cornish cultural identity, those aspects of 'difference' re-emphasised and articulated were often figments of the suburban Englishman's imagination rather than pre-existing elements in the Cornish culture. The Cornish began to be viewed through an exaggerated prism of romantic bourgeois sensibilities;

> the Cornish are an emotional, literal people with no art of their own through which to free themselves; these compensations (religion and/or drink) have therefore become necessary to balance the psychological conflict set up by the severity, insecurity and peninsular nature of their lives . . . this has bred an hard, mercenary, suspicious, clannish, but independent and vivid race of people, who are, however, kind and helpful to one another and show fine qualities among themselves. In spite of their hidebound morality they have a profound love of the fields and the sea.[43]

At least this - from a member of the artists' colony - contains elements that Cornish people might admit have a certain, if tenuous, link with reality. Guide-book writers, however, did not feel it necessary to restrict themselves even this much. Near Launceston, wrote one, 'a road mender was cooking his meal over a fire of sticks, and the smoke, ascending in great clouds, was like an offering of incense to the old gods, the saints, and the fairies of the magic county of the west'.[44] This glorious nonsense appeared in 1934, when male unemployment at Gunnislake, just 20 miles to the south, was a staggering 60%! An extraordinary credibility gap had emerged between the Cornwall of popular fancy and the reality of socio-economic despair, and certainly Cornwall was being re-defined in the interests of tourism. It was becoming picturesque, its towns and villages quaint, its people moody, mystical, superstitious and childlike by turns. This was adding a 'symbolic repertoire' but it was not a repertoire that had much meaning for Cornish popular culture. While the Cornish working class largely ignored it, it was nevertheless significant in that large chunks of the meanings constructed by it were incorporated into English middle-class culture, linking with romanticised notions of the countryside and the traditional.

The production of a set of guide-book meanings of Cornwall has been described as a 'guide-book culture'.[45] But this process is probably best seen as part of a more general emerging service-class culture based on the South East of England.[46] From within this culture the countryside is a place of retreat, simplicity and innocence, peopled by bucolic, smiling villagers. It is a place to be 'discovered', to 'fall in love with' and then to cherish - preferably in the state it was when first found. It is essentially a tamed countryside that is nevertheless 'deep rural England' and it links with the concept of an idealised past as 'heritage'. From within this culture, Cornwall can become a museum of potentially saleable heritage artefacts. Indeed, the 1990s have already seen two tentative proposals for parts of Cornwall to be declared 'world heritage sites'. As this culture penetrated the mass media and became dominant during the 1970s and 80s, it came into conflict with Cornish culture on numerous occasions. Mutual incomprehension sometimes ensued, as when the West Country Tourist Board apparently seriously requested Cornish District Councils to provide lists of local 'characters' for inclusion in their guide-books, only to be met with incredulity.[47] Indeed, perhaps the major challenge faced by bodies such as the Kerrier Groundwork Trust (and its 'Mineral Tramways Project') or the Trevithick Trust (with its key role in re-opening Geevor Tin Mine as a tourist attraction) is in the choice they must make between, on the one hand, the perpetuation on the grand scale of this 'guide-book culture' view of Cornwall and, on the other, the creation of an authentic reflection of Cornwall's past with which Cornish people can identify.

While the guide-book imagery has provided another way of reading Cornwall, the 20th century has also seen an indigenous attempt to recreate Cornish culture. In the late 19th century the first stirrings of the Cornish Revival could be heard. This was a conscious project on the part of a small fraction of the Cornish middle class to solve the problems caused by the collapse of industrial Cornwall. Instead of focusing on the lost glories of steam-engine technology, this group began to look to a past when Cornwall was unashamedly 'different', ignoring the more subtle difference of a discredited popular culture. To do so, however, they had to go back at least to before 1537, preferably to the 14th century, when a large proportion of the Cornish people were Cornish speaking, when its churches were Catholic and when the Duchy was the most important political institution in sight.

For the revivalists the most important symbol of Cornishness was the revival of the Cornish language. This had been last spoken colloquially in the fishing villages of West Penwith around 1800. From the 1870s, there had been sporadic interest in its remains and in the many dialect words in the English of West Cornwall, possibly remants of the old tongue. At the turn of the century, this interest was given organisational form, with the short-lived Cowethas Kelto-Kernuak, formed in 1901. The romantic, anti-industrial roots of the founders of the Cowethas is well illustrated by the comments of L.C.Duncombe-Jewell, one of its prime movers: 'I enjoy, with all its drawbacks the Celtic heritage: the love of poetry and colour, the pilgrimage of dreams, the pageant of nature, the devotion to the fixed star of a principle, the desire to pursue ideas to their logical conclusion, no man withstanding'.[48] The early revivalists were attracted to royalism, Catholicism and the Celtic language and looked to

Brittany for their role model. With hindsight, this could hardly have been further from the radical Liberal, Methodist, rugby-watching working-class culture that the Cornish popular identity was based upon. Nevertheless, the early revival did result in the publication of the first handbook of the Cornish language, written by Henry Jenner in 1904 and, largely because of Jenner's advocacy, Cornwall's acceptance into the Celtic Congress around the same time.[49] The Cornish Revival had arrived.

The inter-war years were ones of slow progress for this new sub-culture of Cornishness. Trapped in a linguistic ghetto of their own making, the early revivalists, many of them in exile, found it difficult to make inroads into popular culture. Despite the formation of the Cornish Gorseth in 1928 and a pressure group-cum-language society, Tyr ha Tavas, in 1933, a newspaper correspondent in 1937 correctly stated that 'if we are quite truthful we have to admit that the revival of the Gorsedd [sic] has scarcely touched the lives of the common people in Cornwall.'[50] Attempts at sythesis had been made - notably in the Old Cornwall movement, begun in 1920 at StIves, and led by Robert Morton Nance. But the Old Cornwall societies, while encouraging interest in all aspects of Cornwall's past, never really fulfilled Morton-Nance's hope that they would become the basis of a New Cornwall and a revived, freshly confident Cornish cultural identity. The writings of A.K.Hamilton Jenkin, who popularised Cornish social history and rekindled interest in the classic mining period in the inter-war years, were also, in their own way, an attempt to synthesise the culture of industrialism with the new Cornishness of the revivalists, although ultimately it leant more towards the former than the latter and was in sympathy with the die-hard school of Cornish thought which insisted that the present difficulties were only passing and that the great days of mining and 'industrial prowess' would sooner or later be restored.[51] We can see, therefore, the Cornish intelligentsia in the inter-war years being pulled in two opposing directions - towards the fading glories of the industrial, technocratic Cornish identity of the 19th century on the one hand, and towards the even more remote glories of an unashamedly 'different' and Celtic-Catholic Cornwall of the middle ages on the other.[52] Meanwhile, the increasingly proletarian popular culture continued with its own historical momentum, apparently doomed to extinction and largely untouched by the concerns of the local 'chattering classes'.

MAJORETTE TROUPES AND THE MEXICAN WAVE : A POST-MODERNIST CULTURE IN THE MAKING?

As the British economy began its fundamental shift away from manufacturing towards a service economy around the end of the 1950s, the working-class culture of its industrial areas began to fragment. In Cornwall, too, the working-class popular culture seemed to be threatened, not so much by a decline in the industrial sector - in fact Cornwall had a mini-manufacturing boom from the mid-1960s to 1974, but by a general shift to the service sector together with other social processes. Pre-eminent among these was a growing geographical mobility, which from 1960 heralded the reversal of long established demographic trends and the arrival of a new population, mainly from the South of England and largely unaware of the nature of Cornish culture or its historical and social roots. Together with these demographic factors, the extension of the mass media, bringing the global values of television into the home, and the rise of more affluent, home-centred lifestyles have often been cited as more general forces leading to the breakdown of working class and local cultures. Concentrating on these factors, the mass society theorists of the 1950s and 60s predicted that global values would gradually homogenise society and eradicate the sense of place and local culture. However, this view was soon to be challenged.[53] For example, Savage has argued that the situation is in reality far more complex than this. While many people may lead increasingly uniform lives, with similar leisure pursuits, shopping at identical supermarkets, consuming similar televisual messages, there is at the same time an increased perception of local spatial differences. Somewhat paradoxically, therefore, people can have a greater identification with their 'imagined community' alongside growing spatial uniformity.[54] Amongst other things, this helps to explain the otherwise puzzling upsurge in ethnic identities and even ethnoregional movements in advanced Western societies since the 1960s.

The paradoxical situation noted by Savage has certainly been reflected in post-war Cornwall. To take a localised example, Herman Gilligan has studied cultural change in Padstow. There, he noted the Cornish culture based on a common experience of an informal economy and 'familial and communal support networks which have been developed by Padstonians in the face of adversity'.[55] In this we can observe the familiar culture of making-do. However, in the 1960s this close-knit local culture took on new meaning as the Cornish were consigned to council estates and contrasted their own economic and political powerlessness with the better-off incoming population attracted by Padstow's reputation as a holiday resort. Tourism in fact 'enhanced the cultural significance of what it meant to be "local", and engendered an almost exaggerated sense of Padstonian communal solidarity'.[56] In parallel with this, small-scale industrial investment in the town disturbed the equilibrium of local networks of employment access and gender relations. The sense of 'difference' was thus heightened by social change rather than submerged by it.

The same paradox can be seen occurring on a broader level. After the 1950s, the Cornish Revival began to break out of its ghetto. Firstly, it politicised itself, which helped bring a Cornish dimension back into general Cornish politics, and secondly, some of the cultural symbols that the revivalists had been busily inventing began to percolate into the consciousness of Cornish people in general: notably the flag of St Piran, an awareness of and interest in the revived language, and even a Cornish tartan. At the same time, the reaction of the indigenous Cornish to socio-economic change that was so noticeable at Padstow was replicated throughout Cornwall as people sought strategies to deal with economic disadvantage.

In politics, the growing sense of anti-metropolitanism based on regional under-development which emerged in the 1960s was co-opted by local Liberals and reached its peak in the mass popular support given to David Penhaligon in the later 1970s and early 1980s. Even official bodies began to reflect a changed discourse of local politics. A Cornwall County Council guide could assert in 1988 that 'Cornwall is administratively "in" England, but is not "of" England. Culturally the River Tamar is a national boundary'.[57] The Council's own evidence to the 1988 Inquiry on the Euro-constituency stated that: 'such feelings of loyalty are of a very different order from most counties in England ... It (Cornwall) has a strong separate identity with its own history, tradition, customs, language, and (to some degree) law and institutions. Many of these attributes are firmly rooted in its Celtic past'.[58] Cornish culture seemed to have re-emerged into the public and political domain.

Significantly, the most fervent and determined expressions of this new anti-metropolitanism were reserved for those issues where the territorial integrity of Cornwall was at stake. This was most clearly observed in the (successful) battle to prevent the territorial expansion of Plymouth into South East Cornwall in the local government re-organisation of the early 1970s, and in the campaign to achieve a Cornwall-only Euro-constituency in the 1980s and 1990s. The territorial imperative was also exhibited in renewed demands for the 'accommodation' of Cornwall, from a campaign for a Cornish postage stamp and a brief attempt by the County Council to request a 'Minister for Cornwall', to demands for the reconstitution of the ancient Stannary Parliament and the powers of the Duchy of Cornwall.

Cornwall County Council's attempts to put to the European Community Cornwall's socio-economic case for special and separate treatment also had a strong territorial flavour, noting that 'Many still see Cornwall as having a distinct "national" identity'.[59] Similarly, criticisms in the 1980s that the planning process had failed to take sufficient account of questions of territory, ethnicity and cultural identity[60] had clearly had an impact, the County Council's Structure Plan consultative document in 1993 being entitled *Cornwall: A Land Apart*, its observations based on the premise that 'Cornwall is different'.[61] As Taylor has noted, at root notions of cultural identity are linked inextricably to those of territory.[62] This, of course, helps to explain the destruction of Vukovar or the scramble for central Bosnia, but it also sheds light upon the nature of Cornish anti-metropolitanism. 'Cornwall begins at Tamar!' declared the anti-Tamarside car-stickers of the early 1970s, an indication of the way in which the revivalists had mobilised territory as an effective vehicle for politicisation. The physical territory of Cornwall had, in fact, become an important symbol of cultural identity.

Economically, the rapid changes experienced since 1945 served to exacerbate Cornish 'difference'. Post-war Cornwall became the land not only of tourism but of 'small businesses' (both service and light-manufacturing), with an increasing but not always advantageous reliance on central government regional development policies. Extensive in-migration aggravated an already difficult housing situation, leading to the peculiarly Cornish low-wage / high house-price nexus which had reached acute proportions by the late 1980s. High unemployment rates and the continued emigration of young persons also contributed to the distinctive Cornish economic mix, with many indigenous Cornish people relying increasingly on extended family networks to help alleviate problems of housing and employment. Dunkerly and Wallace noted that young people especially were driven to devise 'coping strategies' to come to terms with their economic situations. This involved 'both formal and informal work practices, casualization and self-employment', with many young Cornish 'socialized into long hours, hard work and poor rewards'.[63] The attitudes and behaviour thus created were to outside observers recognisably 'Cornish', while internally within Cornwall they reinforced the sense of belonging to an imagined Cornish community with its own problems and its own ways of dealing with them.

Socially, the cultural identity again found its expression in the success of the Cornish rugby team after 1988. At first glance, this appeared to be a re-run of the sporadic outbursts of collective popular identity that had marked the years since 1908. However, by the late 1980s, there were significant differences observable in this popular expression of Cornishness. A new synthesis of cultural symbols could be spotted at rugby matches. The spectators had borrowed symbols in a fairly eclectic fashion from a number of different cultures and, in doing so, invested them with Cornish meanings. Traditional symbols of Cornishness such as the song 'Trelawny', the 'obby' oss and pasties were joined in 1990 at Redruth by the Mexican wave, adopted from televised World Cup soccer, and demonstrated with extraordinary self-confidence by the 40,000 Cornish who witnessed their team's victory at Twickenham in 1991.

More interesting, perhaps, is the way in which symbols from the Cornish Revival were also mixed unselfconsciously with the older popular symbols; for example, the widespread use of the black and white StPirans Cross, and even the Cornish language - in the willingness to use 'Kernow', the Cornish word for Cornwall. The crucial strategic role of the Cornish Revival in this process should be stressed. It provided new symbols for popular culture, reinforcing the Cornish sense of cultural 'difference', giving it visible meaning and self-confidence. The re-appearance of the 'Cornish novel' in the 1980s and 1990s, in the work of N.R.Phillips, Myrna Combellack and Alan Kent, was further evidence of this process, although their work still had the strong fatalist edge familar from early 20th century popular culture.[64] Nevertheless, the popular culture was being articulated once again, and had moved into a more dynamic phase.

CONCLUSION

What all the above suggests for the future is difficult to predict. We can conclude that Cornish culture has a persistent meaning for a large proportion of the population of Cornwall but it is changing in unforeseen ways. The sense of belonging to an imagined Cornish community now rests on a wider set of symbols than before; a changing repertoire which includes co-opted elements from other cultures and newly re-invented 'traditions'. Perhaps to future generations, majorette troupes, very popular in the 1990s among Cornish communities in the Camborne-Redruth area, and the Mexican wave, will be seen as being as 'Cornish' as pasties, saffron buns or the mining heritage. This may only be a case of any symbol in a storm, or it could be testament to a re-invigorated and still dynamic sense of Cornish cultural identity. The evidence, we would venture to suggest, points to the latter.

NOTES AND REFERENCES

1. Denis Cosgrove, 'And now we take Berlin. . .', *Journal of Historical Geography*, 1990.
2. For the concept of maps of meanings see A.P.Cohen, *Belonging*, Manchester, 1983; Peter Jackson, *Maps of Meaning*, London, 1989; Nigel Thrift, 'Images of social change', in Chris Hamnett, Linda McDowell, Philip Sarre [eds], *The Changing Social Structure*, London, 1989.
3. For example Rosalie Eastlake, 'Cornwall : the Development of a Celtic Periphery', unpublished MA Thesis, McGill University, 1981; Peter Berresford Ellis, *The Celtic Revolution*, Talybont, 1985.
4. Gill Burke, 'The Cornish Miner and the Cornish Mining Industry : 1870-1921', unpublished PhD Thesis, University of London, 1981; Bernard Deacon, 'Cornish Culture or the Culture of the Cornish?', *Cornish Scene*, NS1 1988, pp. 58-60; Bernard Deacon, Andrew George, Ronald Perry, *Cornwall at the Crossroads*, Redruth, 1988 (chapter 14); J.Herman Gilligan, 'The Rural Labour Process : a Case Study of a Cornish Town', in Tony Bradley and Philip Lowe [eds], *Locality and Rurality: Economy and Society in Rural Regions'* Norwich, 1984; Philip Payton, 'Modern Cornwall, the Changing Nature of Peripherality', unpublished PhD thesis, Polytechnic South West, 1989; Tony Rallings and Adrian Lee, 'Politics of the Periphery - the Case of Cornwall?', paper presented to Conference of the PSA, Aberystwyth, 1977; Mary McArthur, 'The Cornish: A Case Study in Ethnicity', unpublished MSc thesis, University of Bristol, 1988.
5. This article draws extensively upon Payton (1989), which provides a comprehensive historical framework for the development of Cornish culture. See also Philip Payton, *The Making of Modern Cornwall: Historical Experience and the Persistence of 'Difference'*, Redruth, 1992.
6. Raymond Williams, *Marxism and Literature*, Oxford, 1977.
7. John Rowe, *Cornwall in the Age of the Industrial Revolution*, Liverpool, 1953, re-published, St Austell, 1993.
8. For the middle class reaction to the culture of industrialism see Denise Crook, 'The Early History of the Royal Geological Society of Cornwall', unpublished PhD thesis, Open University, 1990 and A.C.Todd, *Beyond the Blaze; a Biography of Davies Gilbert*, Truro, 1967.
9. Davies Gilbert [ed], *Mount Calvary*, London, 1826, p. v.
10. Heard's *Gazetteer of the County of Cornwall*, Truro, 1817.
11. Thomas Quiller-Couch, 'Bodmin Riding and Halgaver Sports', *Journal of the Royal Cornwall Polytechnic Society*, 1864.2, pp. 56-60.
12. Payton, 1989, p. 147; Payton, 1992, p. 77.
13. R.Warner, *A Tour through Cornwall*, Bath, 1809, p. 348.
14. Burke, 1981, pp. 288ff and 331ff.
15. For evidence of the persistence of local customs and folk tales, see William Botterell, *Traditions and Hearthside Stories of West Cornwall*, Penzance, 1870-1880 and Robert Hunt, *Popular Romances of the West of England*, London, 1865.
16. Doreen Massey, *Spatial Divisions of Labour*, London, 1984, provides a model of how uneven development produces cultural and social change.
17. Mervyn Davy, *Hengan*, Redruth, 1980.

18. H.D.Lowry, *Wheal Darkness*, London, 1902.
19. Philip Payton, *The Cornish Miner in Australia*, Redruth, 1984; Oswald Pryor, *Australia's Little Cornwall*, Adelaide, 1962.
20. Payton, 1989, p. 206; Payton, 1992, pp. 112-113.
21. Payton, 1984, p. 210.
22. Burke, 1981, p. 330.
23. Burke, 1981, p. 331.
24. Henry Harris, *The Luck of Wheal Vor*, Truro, 1901.
25. Burke, 1981, p. 347.
26. *West Briton*, 24th March, 1903.
27. Payton, 1989, p. 210; Payton, 1992, p. 114.
28. Harris, 1901.
29. H.D.Lowry, *Wreckers and Methodists*, London, 1893.
30. Quoted in Denys Val Baker, *The Spirit of Cornwall*, London, 1980, p. 16.
31. D.H. Lawrence, 'Samson & Delilah', in *England, My England*, London, 1992.
32. *Cornish Leaders*, 1935.
33. For a comparative 'making-do' culture, see Pauline Barner, 'Culture, Capital and Class Conflicts in the Political Economy of Cape Breton', *Journal of Historical Sociology*, 3.4, 1990, pp. 362-378.
34. *West Briton*, 29th December 1921.
35. For example A.K.Hamilton Jenkin, *The Cornish Miner*, London, 1927.
36. Fortescue Hitchens and Samuel Drew, *The History of Cornwall. volume 1*, Helston, 1824, p. 710.
37. Hitchens and Drew, 1824, p. 711.
38. Tom Salmon, *The First 100 years; the Story of Rugby Football in Cornwall*, Illogan, 1983.
39. J.C. Trewin, *Up From the Lizard*, London, 1948, republished 1982, p. 197.
40. Payton, 1989, p. 291; Payton, 1992, pp. 151-159
41. Arthur Quiller-Couch, *Cornish Magazine. volume 1*, 1898, p. 237.
42. J.Urry, *Holidaymaking: Cultural Change and the Seaside*, Lancaster Regional Group Working Paper No.22, 1987.
43. Sven Berlin, *Horizons*, 1943
44. F.I.Cowles, *The Magic of Cornwall*, London, 1934, p. 218.
45. Deacon *et al.*, *Cornwall at the Crossroads*, Redruth, 1988, p. 105.
46. Thrift, 1989.
47. *West Briton*, 10th September 1987.
48. L.C.Duncombe-Jewell, 'About myself and the Celtic-Cornish movement', *The Candid Friend and Traveller*, July 5th 1902, pp. 399-400.
49. Henry Jenner, *Handbook of the Cornish Language*, London, 1904.
50. Quoted in Payton, 1989, p. 249; Payton, 1992, p. 135.
51. A.K.Hamilton Jenkin, 1927.
52. Payton, 1989, p. 239; 1992, p. 130.
53. See John Clarke, '"There's no place like…": cultures of difference', in John Allen and Doreen Massey [eds], *Geography Matters!*, Cambridge, 1984.
54. Mike Savage, 'Spatial Differences in Modern Britain', in Hamnett *et al.*, 1989, pp. 244-268.
55. Gilligan, 1984.
56. Gilligan, 1984.
57. Ivan Rabey [ed.], Cornwall. *An Official Guide*, Truro, *c*.1988, p. 31.
58. Cornwall County Council's submission to the public inquiry into the Euro-Constituency, 1988.
59. Cornwall County Council, Devon County Council, Plymouth City Council, *Towards an Economic Strategy for Cornwall and Devon*, 1992, p. 14.
60. Deacon *et al.*, 1988.
61. Cornwall County Council, *Cornwall: A Land Apart - Issues for the New Structure Plan*, Truro, 1993, p. 1.
62. Peter J. Taylor, 'The meaning of the North: England's "foreign country" within?', *Political Geography*, Vol 12, No2, March 1993.

63. David Dunkerley and Claire Wallace, 'Young People and Employment in the South West', in Philip Payton (ed.), *Journal of Interdisciplinary Economics*, Vol 4., No 3, 1992.
64. Myrna Combellack, *The Playing Place*, Redruth, 1989; N.R.Phillips, *The Saffron Eaters*, Exeter, 1987; Alan Kent, *Clay*. Launceston, 1991.

CORNWALL AND CHANGES IN THE 'TOURIST GAZE'

Paul Thornton

INTRODUCTION

Cornwall has long been recognised as one of the United Kingdom's most important and distinctive tourist areas. It has regularly attracted over three million tourists a year, peaking at 3.4 million in 1978.[1] This importance as a holiday destination led Cornwall County Council to state that:

> The characteristics of the County - in particular its coastal scenery and climate - are such that it has become one of the most popular holiday areas in the United Kingdom, and this is an important way in which Cornwall makes its contribution to the life of the country as a whole. The lives of many of the nation's people are refreshed and enriched through their holiday experience of Cornwall.[2]

Cornwall County Council may see Cornwall as an important contributor to the life of the country as a whole, but this is matched by the importance of tourism to the Duchy's economy. The three million visitor figure is generally recognised as the minimum number of visitors necessary to sustain the industry in its present form. The Cornwall Tourist Visitor Survey in 1992[3] estimated that the average spent per visitor to be £254, and from this general figure it is easy to estimate the contribution of tourism to Cornwall's economy as £726 million per annum.[4]

Clearly, therefore, any general trends in the development of tourism are likely to be of specific importance to the economy of Cornwall. It is the purpose of this article to examine the extent to which recent trends identified in the UK tourist industry as a whole can be seen as relevant to the Cornish situation. To achieve this, it is necessary to look at the changing experiences of the UK and Cornish tourist industries through the twentieth century, the period in which mass-tourism developed.[5] But to understand the significance of recent trends

80

it is also important to examine the theoretical background and previous studies relating to these developments. Initially, Jafari's major review article on the sociocultural dimensions of tourism will be considered, followed by the theoretical contributions to the study of tourism and leisure made by Urry in his postulation of the 'tourist gaze'.

THEORETICAL CONSIDERATIONS

As part of his large English language review of the theoretical debates concerning tourism, Jafari found it necessary to examine the nature of the tourist industry. He argued that tourism 'is *not* an independent event but is part of and a means to other ends. In other words, tourism is an integral part of the tourist-generating and-receiving systems.'[6] That is, tourism could be visualized as a system, consisting primarily of the interactions of two sub-systems, one of which generates tourists and the other which caters for their needs. For the sake of clarity it is best to consider the two sub-systems separately. The generating system 'nurtures' and 'breeds' tourists through its actions on its individuals.[7] The generating system can be a country, a state or even a city (depending on the definition of its boundaries). While the purpose of this system is to serve its people (workers), its operation has become so important to them that it has risen above them. Krippendorf argues that they actually work for the system, and that its operation drains them both mentally and physically. This drain is so serious that they cannot adequately perform their roles in a sub-optimal condition. As Jafari has commented,

> Therefore, it (the generating system) must annex 're-creative' sub-systems or satellites for the treatment of 'exertions' and 'anomalies' cumulated in its ordinary system . . . . When the process is complete, they are ready to resume their positions back home . . . .[8]

Krippendorf believes the same but is characteristically blunter: 'We work in order to go on holiday, among other things, and we need holidays in order to be able to work again'.[9] The cure for the exertions that tourists have been subjected to varies according to the patient and the recreative sub-system available. However, if the generating system is the 'ordinary world' of the tourist, then the receiving sub-system must be in comparison 'non-ordinary'. In other words, tourist destinations must be 'different'.

It is fairly clear, then, that the annexing of tourist satellites (or receiving sub-systems) is in the interests of the generating sub-system. Without this externalization, the generating sub-system may well 'burn-out' due to accumulated stress and inefficiency. But it should be noted that the receiving sub-system 'by taking the heat off the tourist generators may add to its own or absorb beyond its capacity . . . which . . . may lead to a burn-out not totally of its own making.'[10] Krippendorf summarises the theory quite neatly, stating that: 'Tourism is social therapy, the valve that maintains the world in good running order.'[11]

The idea that the tourist is seeking the 'non-ordinary' in order to recuperate from the mental and physical drain that the system in which he lives imposes upon him can be related to the work of Urry on the 'tourist gaze'. In the *Tourist Gaze*, Urry emphasized what he saw as the fundamentally visual nature of tourism.[12] Intuitively, such a claim seems one-sided, since it is quite obvious that tourists take part in all kinds of activities when away from home. However, Urry has responded that:

> It was never my intention to suggest that other senses are not stimulated on holiday. Tourists experience extremes of heat, taste unexpected dishes, experience heightened passions, hear unusual sounds, encounter new smells, and so on. Rather, my claim was that these experiences are only of importance to the tourist because they are located within a distinctive visual environment. It is the unusualness of the visual sensations that places these other activities within a different frame.[13]

Visual consumption is not a simple process but one that involves the collection of distinctive 'signs' by the tourist. Such signs might include, for example, the seeing of a wholly unique object, such as Buckingham Palace, the signifier of British monarchy and empire, or the Empire State Building, the original signifier of American corporate power. Alternatively, the search for signs can be more subtle - a good example might be the attempts to find true 'olde England'. The main thrust of Urry's work has been to demonstrate that in tourism there should be something distinctive or unusual to gaze upon - that is, the signs that the tourist 'collects' must be visually extraordinary. It is this that provides the tourist with an experience that is out of the ordinary and separated from the mundane of everyday life. This, Jafari and Krippendorf agree, is the essence of tourism.[14]

What the tourist chooses to gaze upon is, according to Urry,[15] dependent very much on the society in which he normally exists. In fact, the nature of the ordinary world is critical in determining the definition of what compromises the non-ordinary. In many ways, the generating system is the physical embodiment of the ordinary world, and would, therefore, be one of the bench-marks that the tourist would use when searching for the non-ordinary in which to relax. If the society that generates the tourist changes, then the nature of tourism will adjust as a result. It is to these developments in UK tourism in the twentieth century, and the changes in the nature of the society that spawned it, that attention will now be turned.

DEVELOPMENT OF MASS-TOURISM IN THE UK

The development of seaside tourism, and the social changes that encouraged it, are the subject of two important books by Walvin, *Leisure and Society* and *Beside the Seaside*.[16] In these books, Walvin argues that prior to the 19th century there had been the development of towns whose specific purpose was recreational - on the whole, inland spa towns. The only members of society who were able to take advantage of these were the well-off. However,

> By the early years of the 19th century urban England was changing rapidly; not only were there towns given over the pursuit of leisure, but well away from the spas were towns whose sole function and rationale was work. The industrial towns of the nineteenth century, which in the formative years denied leisure of most kinds to their labour force, were as characteristic of the new century as were the spas of the eighteenth; the one built for work, the other for rest.....Substantial numbers of city dwellers began to turn to nearby seaside towns for an escape, however brief, from the cities .....[17]

Two factors stimulated this drift to the seaside. The first was contemporary medical opinion that saw salt-water as a cure for many ills; under careful medical supervision of course! The second element was royal example, and the desire to emulate it. The switch of allegiance from inland to the coast was, therefore, part medically-inspired and part social fad.

However, this coastal tourism was not what we today would understand as 'seaside tourism'. It was restricted to the wealthier classes, and later the developing middle class anxious to follow their example. Poorer people also had a high opinion of the value of bathing but spatial distance and high travel costs meant they were unable to go to these coastal areas. It took the arrival of the railway, 'the fruit and the cause of industrial change',[18] to allow them also to escape briefly from the cities. The demand was released, and the results were impressive. For example, in Whit-week in 1850, 200,000 Manchester residents left by train for the seaside. The coastal towns, used to dealing with an upper-class customer, were decidedly shocked. Walvin quotes a contemporary newspaper to illustrate this: 'Unless immediate steps are taken, Blackpool as a resort for respectable visitors will be ruined .... . Unless the cheap trains are discontinued or effective regulation made for the management of the thousands who visit the place, Blackpool property will be depreciated past recovery'.[19]

The coastal resorts found themselves much in demand, but that demand was not uniform, and varied across the social spectrum:

> The outcome (of the high opinion of the restorative qualities of the sea) was that the seaside developed an attraction (resistable only by the very poor) for all classes of English society. To working people with time and money it afforded a welcome, pleasurable, though all-too-brief escape for a day or two from an unhealthy industrial atmosphere. For the middle classes and their

superiors it provided either a suburb-by-the-sea or a peaceful
retreat into retirement and, with luck, better health.[20]

This large demand meant that the major resorts began developing into
centres of pleasure, offering to the long-stay or casual visitor more than just the
simple benefits of beach and sea. To Walvin these new seaside centres
epitomised the commercialisation of leisure as a whole in Britain.

How does this link with Jafari's theory of generating and recreative sub-
systems, and Krippendorf's views on the strains of modern living? It is the
change in the nature of work that is important. Walvin argues that it had not
mattered that mainly agricultural workers took refuge from their work in the
only way they could afford and was available to them - alcohol. A loss of
efficiency due to over-work or the after-effects of alcohol was not critical. In
the new industrial age, however, such a condition was inconvenient for the
employer and dangerous in the new factory environment. The value of the
holiday, made newly-available by the same technological changes, became
clear, so that:

> By the early years of the twentieth century . . . the concept of
> holidays with pay had become an increasingly common union
> demand and was to be found as an increasingly common concession
> offered by management . . . . The numbers of firms providing
> holidays with pay steadily grew, though usually linked to an
> insistence on prompt and regular attendance through the rest of
> the working year[21]

This new attitude was reflected in the decision of the Trades Union
Congress after 1911 to press for annual holidays with pay for all workers.
However, this long sought-after legislation did not appear until 1938, and even
then it was delayed until the late 1940s.

Having examined the conditions that encouraged the development of
seaside resorts near industrial towns, attention will now be turned to the more
distant destination of Cornwall.

DEVELOPMENT OF MASS-TOURISM IN CORNWALL

Walvin mentions Cornwall only once, in his otherwise detailed examination of
mass-tourism *Beside the Seaside*, remarking briefly:

> Some resorts (Bournemouth being perhaps the best example)
> whose railway links came late, or which were too distant for
> effective day-trips, were able to maintain their social aloofness
> and preserve themselves for visitors of a better sort. From
> Bournemouth west into Devon and Cornwall this tended to be the
> pattern, and poorer visitors did not, in general, break through into

that preserve of the wealthier and the middle-class sick and old, until the inter-war years.[22]

Although it had possessed its own internal industrial railway network for many years, Cornwall was the last county to be connected to the main railway system; as late as 1859.[23] It was not until the early-twentieth century that the full blast of change associated with the railways was felt in Cornwall, with the introduction by the Great Western Railway Company of the 'Cornish Riviera Express'. This reduced the time taken to reach Penzance from Paddington to only seven hours and opened-up Cornwall to the visitor, and was according to Simmons 'a brilliant stroke of publicity'.[24] The notion of 'Riviera' was used successfully to associate Cornwall with foreign countries, in particular Italy and Brittany. The impact of this very imaginative marketing was an increase in railway passenger receipts of almost 71% between 1903 and 1913.[25]

As more people came on holiday to Cornwall, its resort areas began to transform their economies, moving swiftly towards service activities. In Newquay and Penzance employment in personal services accounted for 29.4% and 22.6% of their occupied population in 1921, as compared to a national average of 11.7%.[26] The pace of this development was also reflected in the levels of population growth in the Cornish coastal parishes, which exceeded the average for Cornwall as a whole. Between 1921 and 1931 coastal parishes grew by 3.2% compared to the Cornish average of 0.7%.[27] The majority of the expanding populations were in-migrants attracted to the job opportunities in the growing tourist industry, while others were part of the influx of older retired people (continuing, in a modified form, the well-established trend of health tourism). The members of this group could be best described as 'permanent tourists'.

As a result of being a 'late-starter' in the mass-tourism business, Cornwall developed an intriguing mix of tourist destinations. Bennett, for example, proposed a threefold classification of destination areas within Cornwall, comprising:

(a) New holiday towns, such as Bude and Newquay, which were small coastal settlements that had developed to such an extent that the original nuclei had been reduced to insignificance.
(b) Old ports, fishing centres or towns, which were settlements that had 'an important tourist interest',[28] such as Penzance, Padstow and St Ives.
(c) Groupings of modern buildings, often collections of hotels, holiday homes or other forms of accommodation (later including caravan and camping sites). Between 1954 and 1964, for example, the number of static caravans in Cornwall increased by 240%.[29]

In summary, then, the Cornish experience to some extent reflected national trends. However, the late arrival of the railway ensured that Cornwall catered for the elite market for much longer than was usual elsewhere, with mass-tourism being a relatively late development. The extent to which this has had an enduring influence upon the trends that Cornwall has experienced more recently, compared to national trends, will now be assessed.

RECENT CHANGES IN THE NATURE OF TOURISM WITHIN THE UK

In an article on the social and spatial aspects of services, Urry asks why so many people have now come to see the spending of a week or fortnight's holiday at a traditional UK holiday resort as a much less attractive touristic experience than hitherto, particularly when compared to the decades around the Second World War.[30] The answer would appear to be that there has been a retreat from the idealised view of the seaside holiday as the dominant form of holiday-making, to its being seen as only one of a number of potential activities.

Urry claims that the explanation for this answer must lie in the process of cultural and socio-economic transformation. The development of mass-tourism was, as Walvin demonstrated, a result of changes in society that led to the eclipse of elitist tourism. According to Urry, 'very broadly "mass holiday-making" to the British seaside resort was the quintessential form of tourism in industrial society'.[31] By its very nature mass-tourism was a leisure activity that presupposed regulated and organized work. Thus, with the development of a post-industrial society it is no surprise that new forms of tourism should develop in response, and that in certain important respects these should be different to previous forms of tourism. For Urry, this was the era of 'post-tourism'.

The evidence for this change is to be found amidst various developments. Firstly, the 'ordinary world' of the tourist, that is the generating sub-systems, is no longer dominated by traditional smokestack industries. As a result, the traditional tourism destination areas have become less extraordinary in comparison. In addition, Urry argues that the resorts have suffered from a lack of public and private investment: 'Indeed, the historic absence of a manufacturing base in such towns, combined with the fact that much of the building in such resorts is less than 100 years old, means that there is something of an absence of "interesting", well-preserved sights which can be made sacred, packaged and viewed'.[32]

The latter years of the twentieth century have seen the steady deindustrialisation of many British towns, with the workforce increasingly involved in service provision rather than manufacturing. At the same time, towns which were heavily industrialised have become potential objects of the 'tourist gaze', as demonstrated by the recent success of Bradford in attracting visitors.[33] 'Old resorts' (which are in reality fairly recent constructions) are no longer extraordinary at all, particularly if they lack the interesting 'authentic' objects from the manufacturing past. These traditional holiday resort areas were constructed to offer services (such as amusements and theatres/cinemas) that the mass-tourist was not usually able to experience at home, together with the simpler pleasures of swimming and the beach. This degree of service provision was an important part of the 'extra-ordinary' flavour of these receiving sub-systems, something that has been lost now that most British towns and most British workers are also in the business of service provision. That is, the generating sub-system of the tourist has been transformed to such an extent that the traditional destination area is becoming 'more ordinary'. As Urry noted in his article 'Some Social and Spatial Aspects of Services' the provision of entertainment services, which in the past was concentrated in coastal areas, has been levelled by new developments (in particular television). To make matters worse, the generally small size of the resorts means that they are unable to sustain a very wide range of services, and those they do possess tend to be 'nothing special'.[34] At the same time, paradoxically, areas that were once the generating systems of an industrial society, and now have been abandoned through economic change, have become examples of the extraordinary. The result of this change can be seen in the decision to declare 1993 'Industrial Heritage Year'. It is also reflected in the decision by English Heritage (a government institution set up to bring about the preservation of the non-ordinary) to publish articles in its magazine advocating 'Grand Tours' of industrial England, these juxtaposed alongside the more usual articles on the countryside and stately homes.[35]

To place too much emphasis on the importance of social trends would be to ignore other changes that have been of critical importance - such as changes in technology. Laws, in his book *Tourism Marketing,* argues: 'Technical developments have played a significant role in the increased variety of tourism services and destinations offered'.[36] They have, he concludes, resulted in travel costs falling and becoming a smaller proportion of the total holiday cost. In addition 'point to point' speed has increased, which allows a wider choice of destinations within an identical time budget (assuming that time is a limiting factor). This technical change is not stressed by Urry, yet it should not be ignored. Technical change could mean that tourists are discriminating against British resorts because of their lack of guaranteed sun (one aspect of the 'tourist gaze' these resorts are unable to supply).

The apparent decline and fall of the British seaside holiday from its pre-eminent position should be set alongside other information. In the 1990s the majority of holiday-makers choose Mediterranean sunbelt destinations, whereas as recently as 1965 British resorts dominated - eight out of ten chose a UK holiday. Yet British residents engaging in 'tourist trips' in the UK in 1990, spent an extraordinary £7,350 million.[37] The apparent growth of tourism within the UK at the same time as the demise of the traditional resort areas implies that the British tourist industry is not simply declining but is restructuring in response to changes in the demands made upon it.

The nature of this restructuring is complicated. For example, although the proportion of the adult population taking holidays has scarcely changed since the mid-1960s (remaining at six out of ten since the 1970s), the number of adults taking more than one holiday a year has more than trebled.[38] It is wrong, therefore, to assume that all elements of society equally form the demand for tourism. For example, in the past only the wealthy could travel, while later the middle class also gained the ability, and later still the skilled working class used the railway to escape the ordinary world. Thus Prentice has shown that in 1989 households with an average weekly income of £225-£274 spent the national average amount on hotels and holiday expenses. Households with an average weekly income of between £100-£124 spent on average only one third of the national average on hotels and holiday expenses, while households with an average weekly income of between £80-£99 spent only one tenth of the average on these services. In contrast, the richer end of society (such as those with weekly incomes of £550-£624) spent twice the national average, and those with weekly incomes of £750+ spent an amazing four times the national average.

It is not enough to merely examine the financial ability to travel. The purpose that tourism serves must also be addressed. The development of the 'yuppie' lifestyle was seen as an important factor by Williams and Shaw. This lifestyle was,

> a bipolarized combination of high-flying and highly pressurized work with conspicuous, hedonistic consumption. Tourism was one of the more visible symbols of the latter. With the simple ability to travel to foreign destinations long having been relegated to the realms of mass tourism, aspiring yuppies used tourism in new ways to demarcate their social position and 'extraordinary' lifestyle. In particular frequency of vacation (second, third, and fourth breaks being commonplace) and distinctiveness in terms of destinations were the tourism hallmark of this group.[39]

Importantly, the activities of this one social group tended to be reflected, albeit in a more dilute form, across the other social strata. These changes were reflected in Prentice's work on average earnings and tourism spending. Shaw and Williams drew particular attention to the development of the 'travel portfolio', in which:

> A weekend walking the hills or experiencing a historic city often rounded out a portfolio for a privileged elite, which might also include 10 days of skiing and 2 weeks in Thailand. Lower down the social scale it might be day excursions to nearby attractions that rounded out a portfolio centred on 2 weeks of sunshine in Florida or the Mediterranean region.[40]

It is this search for new locations to round off a travel portfolio that has helped to encourage the development of tourism involving what Prentice describes as 'heritage features'.[41] He showed, for example, that Wales as a tourist destination had many negative perceptions attached to it as a main destination, but as a location for a secondary holiday it was associated with a sense of history, peace, and fresh air and health.

Other signs of the increase in interest in heritage features are demonstrated by Feist and Hutchinson in their book *Cultural Trends in the 1980s*.[42] What they found particularly striking was the dramatic growth in the membership of some of the main heritage organisations, especially the National Trust. The membership of the National Trust had in fact grown exponentially, as is shown in figure 1.1.

FIGURE 1.1
MEMBERSHIP OF VOLUNTARY HERITAGE ORGANISATIONS

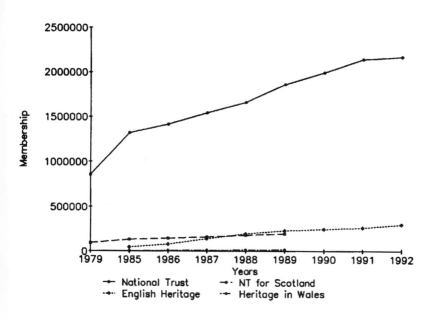

Source: Feist and Hutchinson 1990, English Heritage 1992, National Trust Annual Report 1991.

This increased interest in heritage as a tourist attraction, led Lowenthal to conclude that: 'If the past is a foreign country, nostalgia has made it the foreign country with the healthiest tourist trade of all'.[43]

RECENT CHANGES IN THE NATURE OF TOURISM WITHIN CORNWALL

Perhaps the most significant trend to interest a regional tourism industry is the variation in the number of visitors attracted to its destination area. Within

Cornwall the trend has been broadly one of increasing visitor numbers since the mid-19th century, with the major growth commencing in the 1950s.[44] Between 1954 and 1974 the number of visitors to the Duchy more than doubled from 1.41 million to 3.08 million. (See Figure 1.2). Since this high-point, visitor numbers have declined or at best stagnated, with 3.43 million in 1978 and 3.25 million in 1985: 'Nevertheless, in most years it still ranks third amongst UK counties in terms of the number of tourists it attracts'.[45]

FIGURE 1.2
NUMBER OF VISITORS IN CORNWALL

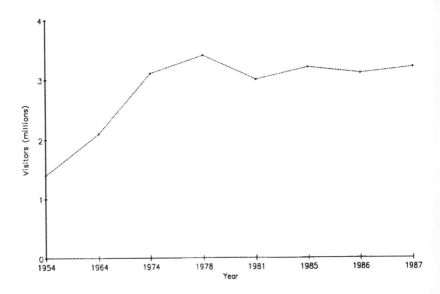

Source: Cornwall County Council Planning Department.

Cornwall appears to be experiencing, in accordance with the national trend, a decline in the numbers of visitors arriving in its traditional destinations. Despite a climate superior to that of the rest of the UK, Cornwall still lacks the element of guaranteed sun. However, these broad trends tend to over-generalise the actual situation, which is considerably more complicated, with variations occurring in Cornwall according to sub-areas. Williams *et al.* believe there are important contrasts between 'mass' tourist resorts such as Newquay and St Ives, and large numbers of small but attractive coastal villages such as Port Isaac which tend to cater for small, more elitist market segments.[46]

These trends appear to concur with Urry's proposal that the mass-tourist of the industrial society is being replaced by the post-tourist of the post-industrial society. The experiences of the Welsh Tourist Board, described earlier, that as a main holiday destination Wales creates negative perceptions, yet as an additional holiday destination it is competitively strong, could be true to some extent of Cornwall, given its sense of history and natural beauty. The greatest problem in analysing such changes in tourist demand in Cornwall is a lack of suitable data. Some information can, however, be gathered from two sources - the Cornwall Tourist Visitor Surveys, and known visitor numbers to attractions in Cornwall.

The Cornwall Tourist Visitor Survey is a large questionnaire survey based upon two sub-samples - one based on visitors attending attractions and one on visitors staying in accommodation.[47] The survey has been taken every year since 1987, and so offers a valuable data-source not available for many other tourist areas.

The survey's first result of interest was that nearly 70% of visitors in Cornwall in 1991 were found to be on their main holiday. Approximately a third of visitors were from higher or lower professional/managerial occupations, although this had fallen from previous years. The trends, therefore, seem quite ambiguous. Cornwall is still getting a good percentage of main holiday-makers, although it should be remembered that overall visitor numbers are falling, while those who took their secondary holidays in Cornwall may have visited Cornwall before the study period of the survey began.

The second result of interest is information on holiday activities. This showed that 'going to the beach' and 'walking around town' were considered the most important holiday activities (74% of visitors stated that they were both fairly or very important). Sightseeing by car was considered important by 72%, with 64% considering shopping and 55% seeing strolling in the countryside as important. Of the 'heritage features' described by Prentice, the most important was visiting historic sites at 38%, although there were several more of less importance. To put this in context, visiting theme parks was considered important by 33%.

More information on what the visitor to Cornwall considers important can be gleaned from looking at what they would wish to be improved. The most suggested improvement was actually 'to do nothing', simply to protect natural beauty (31% of all suggestions). Along the same lines, when asked the question 'Does Cornwall need more theme-parks?' the answer was resounding, with 80.6% saying no.[48] The complexities of the situation are also reflected in the data produced on known visitor numbers by the West Country Tourist Board. The main difficulty in using such data is that the number of attractions prepared to report how many visitors they have had each year is not constant. Thus only very broad conclusions can be drawn.

If a simple count of the number of times a particular category has appeared in the twenty most visited attractions over the period 1982-1990 is taken, some interesting results are produced. The miscellaneous category (including theme-park attractions) appeared on 62 occasions, historic attractions 67 occasions, zoos (including 'sanctuaries') 25 occasions, gardens on 10 occasions and museums on 17. The situation is slightly different when the results are weighed according to the categories relative positions in the charts. In this analysis scores were attached according to position (20 points for the most visited, 1 for the 20th most visited).

The miscellaneous category scored 782 points, historic attractions 697 points, zoos 251 points, gardens 70 points and museums 87 points. In this analysis the miscellaneous category dominates, but not by the margin that might be expected. However, conclusions from this data are limited. For example, the data applies only to managed attractions. Landscape and other spectacles, important in the Cornish context, are not quantified. For example, the development of a theme-park at Land's End does not mean that visitors suddenly took to visiting the location and had not done so before; it only means that they are now able to be recorded. A better way forward would be an investigation into tourist behaviour on holiday, looking in particular at how tourists budget and spend their time. The advantage of this approach is that information on activities is produced for both managed and non-managed attractions. Unfortunately, at present no such study exists.

CASE-STUDY: PENZANCE

An alternative means of examining changes in the 'tourist gaze' in Cornwall is to look at the literature produced by one destination area, and examine the changes in the way it has marketed itself. In this study, the case of Penzance has been selected due to its long history of tourism, and the good survival rate of its past publications. The 1890 *Guide to Penzance* saw Penzance's advantages as being: 'Climatically extremely mild, and suitable for invalids; the situation of the town is extremely mild, and sanitary conditions perfect, having an abundant supply of water from two large reservoirs and large filtering beds about two miles from the town . . . '.[49] The health aspects of tourism were complemented by an in-depth description of two hundred and twenty-two 'antiquities' that would be of interest to the visitor. In 1908 little had changed, except the identification of swimming as a 'noble art', and the first mention of the railway in the guide. Penzance was still seen by the guide writers as being a self-contained resort. By 1926 Penzance was considered as attractive, not because it offered itself as a self-contained resort; quite the opposite, as it was now 'a centre for excursion and exploration', while 'by common consent, one of its most attractive features to the tourist is the advantage Penzance offers as a centre from which to make excursions'.[50] In 1936 the guide writers had responded to the increasing importance of the motor-car as a means of transport, producing both AA and RAC road maps. A new cost-conscious clientele appears to have arrived, with some of the hotels now advertised as having 'The Maximum of Comfort, Minimum of Cost'. This development was reinforced by the appearance of larger numbers of small to medium sized hotels and establishments offering bed and breakfast. Crucially, the transformation of the 'tourist gaze' away from the antiquity towards the beach was nearing completion: 'Clad only in the minimum necessary for decency, one can sprawl in the sun after one's bathe with the utmost benefit'.[51] The very unusual 1949 brochure reinforced this development, and in addition stated: 'that in every way Cornwall is not England . . . an understanding of this aspect of your holiday in Cornwall adds a great deal to the enjoyment of it and gives something of the piquancy of a holiday abroad'.[52]

The concept of a holiday in Cornwall as being something 'different' was a key part of the 1955 guide. To the guide writers Cornwall was indeed a foreign country (an approach first pioneered by the Great Western Railway Company). The holiday-maker, they felt, would: 'feel a tingle of adventure . . . as you are impelled to make a pilgrimage to the uttermost tip of England . . . This is the most dramatic spot in England'.[53] The 1960 guide's first phrase referred to the 'Magic of Cornwall . . .', which offered 'Elusively satisfying holidays'. St Michael's Mount, was a 'Romantic vision . . . a continental fairy castle'.[54] The guide continued, 'and so the ingredients of this "magic" are added - towering cliffs, covered with heather and gorse; wide sandy bays; quaint coves; Mediterranean blue seas; picturesque fishing villages; exotic sub-tropical gardens; with a warmth and colour unparalleled elsewhere in Britain'.[55] The guide writer's summary is again interesting. While sun, sea and surf might be the main reasons for a holiday, a break given over solely to such activities could cause the holiday-maker some guilt: 'When you come to Penzance, you do much more than come to a seaside resort with a beach, a pier and the usual trappings. You find you have come to the gateway to a holiday'.[56]

The 1973 guide described Penzance as the centre of the Cornish Riviera (a term that had not been used so prominently for many years). Penzance was again a sand, sea and sun resort, but with 'an individuality that never fails to appeal',[57] the implication being that too many seaside towns are too similar and that this similarity is cloying. 'The fairy-tale castle that overlooks Mount's Bay from its rocky summit perfectly reflects the unique magical aura of the far west of Cornwall.' So begins the 1981 guide. In many ways it has changed little, Penzance is 'the resort with character'.[58] The emphasis remains on sun, sea and sand, with a section on 'Cornwall's Heritage', including its 'crumbling mineshafts'. The 1988 guide is the last of the run of very similar guides produced throughout the 1970s and much of the 1980s. It shows few changes, apart from a section on the Cornish language. On the whole, it is rather dated. By way of contrast, the guide for 1993 is in a very different format to that of 1988, and the approach is decidedly more modern. For example,

The sunny days have their gorgeous beaches and family happiness . . . . Holiday-makers and local people are spellbound by the richness of the modern tapestry and the antiquities of this magical peninsula . . . . A land of legend and romance, dark and mystery and vibrant colours . . . a land of island beauty.[59]

Co-existing with the usual promotion of the beaches, sea and weather, are new marketing ideas. For example, the Minack theatre is mentioned, food festivals have appeared, the Tate Gallery (at St Ives, not Penzance) is described, as is the area's contribution to Industrial Heritage Year 1993. Penzance is no longer marketed by itself, but as part of the Penwith peninsula. In addition, new key phrases appear: 'retained their character . . . main streets are almost unchanged . . . communities that have retained their rich individuality . . . a living museum . . . rich in the work of the Newlyn artists . . . great writers. . . creative genius . . . West Cornwall . . . Naturally'.[60] In other words, the guide writers of 1993 are engaged in a market responses to changes in the 'tourist gaze' envisaged by Urry.

CONCLUSION

In tourism as in other respects Cornwall has shown itself to be a unique area, and one that does not always conform to expectations. Mass-tourism arrived late in Cornwall, due to the late arrival of the railway. But even when the railway did arrive, Cornwall's peripheral position (relative to London) meant that mass-tourism did not burst upon it, as had happened near the industrial cities. Cornwall remained 'different', its Celtic identity developed by the guide writers and artworkers of the early 20th century into an image of a foreign country. Even at the height of the mass-tourism era, Cornwall always considered itself the destination area with the most 'character'.

Thus the 'tourist gaze' is a useful theoretical starting point for the analysis of tourism within Cornwall. It offers many insights into the society that develops tourism, and the effects that cultural changes have on the experience that the tourist seeks. However, it is not totally without problems in its application. For example, where Cornwall conforms least with the theories of Urry and others is in the assumptions that are made when dealing with the rest of the UK. These assumptions do not hold up to examination in the Cornish context. Urry saw 'traditional resort areas' as relatively new, constructed to fulfil the demands of the mass-tourist, and less appropriate for the post-tourist seeking an additional holiday in an area that has peace, quiet and a sense of imperturbable history. The new tourists areas offering 'heritage' or 'cultural' tourism experiences were seen as being old industrial areas, areas for walking and cities containing large institutions such as industrial museums.

Cornwall, however, does not fit neatly into this system of classification, as it contains many contrasting elements. It has, for example, the beach and the sea for mass-tourism. Yet it also has the antiquities and more recent industrial relics necessary to attract the 'heritage' tourist, its own distinctive cultural events to attract the 'cultural' tourist, and the scenery and solitude to inspire the stressed worker. All of these elements attract consumers seeking different holidays, and all these consumers offer potential markets that the 'traditional holiday resort' would find difficult to attract. Unlike many of the declining traditional resort areas, Cornwall has a whole host of marketing options that will help to ensure its continued importance as a tourist destination - should it choose to develop them.

REFERENCES

1. Information provided by Cornwall County Council, Planning Department.
2. Cornwall County Council, *Cornwall County Structure Plan: Explanatory Memorandum*, Truro, 1981, p. 136.
3. Tourism Research Group, *Cornwall Visitor Survey*, 1992, Exeter, 1992.
4. Tourism Research Group, 1992.
5. J. Walvin, *Leisure and Society*, London, 1978; J. Walvin, *Beside the Seaside*, London, 1978.
6. J. Jafari, 'Sociocultural Dimensions of Tourism: An English Language Review', in Bustrzanowski (ed.), *Tourism as a Factor of Change*, Vienna, 1989, p. 34.
7. Jafari, 1989.
8. Jafari, 1989, p. 35; see also J.Jafari, 'Tourism Models: The Sociocultural Aspects', *Tourism Management*, 8(2), 1987.
9. J. Krippendorf, *The Holiday Makers*, Oxford, 1989, p. xv.
10. Jafari, 1989, p. 35.
11. Krippendorf, 1989, p. xv.
12. J. Urry, *The Tourist Gaze: Leisure and Travel in Contemporary Societies*, London, 1990.
13. J.Urry, 'The Tourist Gaze Revisited', *American Behavioural Scientist*, 36(2), London, 1992.
14. Jafari, 1989; Krippendorf, 1989.
15. Urry, 1990; Urry, 1992; see also J. Urry, 'Some Social and Spatial Aspects of Services Environment and Planning', *Society and Space*, Vol. 5, 1987.
16. Walvin, 1978 (a); Walvin 1978 (b).
17. Walvin, 1978 (a), p. 13.
18. Walvin, 1978, p. 17.
19. Walvin, 1978 (a), citing the *Preston Pilot*, 1851.
20. Walvin, 1978 (a), p. 75.
21. Walvin, 1978 (b), p. 80.
22. Walvin, 1978 (b), pp. 88-9.
23. J. Simmons, 'The Railway in Cornwall 1835-1914', *Journal of the Royal Institution of Cornwall*, 1982.
24. Simmons, 1982.
25. G. Shaw and A. Williams, 'From Bathing Hut to Theme Park: Tourist Development in South-West England', *Journal of Regional Studies*, Vol. 11, No 42, 1991.
26. Shaw and Williams, 1991.
27. Shaw and Williams, 1991.
28. W. Bennett, 'The Origins and Development of the Tourist Industry in Cornwall', *Royal Cornwall Polytechnic Society Annual Report*, 1948.
29. Bennett, 1948.
30. Urry, 1987.
31. Urry, 1990, p. 35.
32. Urry, 1987, p. 20.
33. A. Bruce, 'Urban and Rural Tourism: A case-study of Bradford and Cornwall', *Local Government Policy Making*, 18(4), 1992.
34. Urry, 1987.
35. *English Heritage Magazine*, Issue 21, March 1993.
36. E. Laws, *Tourism and Marketing*, Cheltenham, 1991, p. 27.
37. R. Prentice, *Tourism and Heritage Attractions*, London, 1993.
38. Prentice, 1992; Welsh Tourist Board, 1991.
39. A. Williams and G. Shaw, 'Tourism Research' in *American Behavioural Scientist*, 36, No 2, 1992.
40. Shaw and Williams, 1992, pp. 135-6.

41. Prentice, 1993.
42. A. Feist and R. Hutchison, *Cultural Trends in the Eighties*, London, 1990.
43. D. Lowenthal, *The Past is a Foreign Country*, Cambridge, 1985, p. 4.
44. A. Williams, G. Shaw, and J. Greenwood, 'From tourist to tourism entrepreneur: evidence from Cornwall', *Environment and Planning*, 2, 1989.
45. Williams *et al.*, 1989.
46. Williams *et al.*, 1989.
47. Tourism Research Group, 1991.
48. Tourism Research Group, 1991.
49. *Guides to Penzance*, 1890, p. 2.
50. *Guides to Penzance*, 1926, p. 18.
51. *Guides to Penzance*, 1936, p. 51.
52. *Guides to Penzance*, 1949, p. 29-31.
53. *Guides to Penzance*, 1955, p. 3.
54. *Guides to Penzance*, 1960, p. 5.
55. *Guides to Penzance*, 1960, p. 9.
56. *Guides to Penzance*, 1960, p. 14.
57. *Guides to Penzance*, 1973, p. 3.
58. *Guides to Penzance*, 1981, p. 4.
59. *Guides to Penzance*, 1993.
60. *Guides to Penzance*, 1993.

HOUSING THE CORNISH:
CONTAINING THE CRISIS
Mary Buck, Malcolm Williams, Lyn Bryant

INTRODUCTION

There is an agreement among a number of commentators[1] that there is a crisis in Cornish housing. This is a crisis which is characterised by insufficient affordable housing for a large section of the population and which has been exacerbated by low wage levels, high rates of unemployment and the inflation of the demand for housing by tourism: a demand which squeezes an already small rented sector[2] and helps to raise house prices because buyers are attracted from higher-priced housing areas. However, in spite of the presence, in abundance, of factors in Cornwall which are likely to lead to homelessness, a smaller proportion of people actually report to district councils as homeless than is the case, for example, in the neighbouring counties of Devon or Somerset, even though these counties both have higher wage levels and lower unemployment rates than does Cornwall.[3] Thus while it is not surprising that Cornwall has a housing crisis, it *is* surprising that the crisis has not reached even greater proportions.

A number of writers have attempted to explain why the proportion of homeless people in Cornwall is somewhat smaller than might be expected, and it has been argued that homelessness in Cornwall is relieved both by outward migration and by the actions of kin groups. Cornish out-migrants have been shown to be likely to display characteristics usually associated with housing deprivation, for example they are more likely to be unemployed, to have more than one member of the household seeking work and to be living in overcrowded conditions.[4] Thus out-migration may be seen to be a potentially important factor in 'resolving' housing need and lessening the Cornish housing crisis. The actions of family members have also been seen as crucial. Lambert *et al.*[5] in their study of North Cornwall, for example, mention the importance of members of extended families providing housing-help for each other in 'absorbing' homelessness. These two 'crisis minimising' factors were explored in a small-scale study of housing and households in Cornwall carried out at the

97

University of Plymouth[6] early in 1993 which was funded by a three month grant from the Faculty of Human Sciences. The short-time scale meant that the research took the form of a pilot-study intended to form the basis of a larger scale project. The data obtained by the study in fact provided some interesting insights in a number of areas. This article is concerned with one of these areas: the role played by Cornish families in resolving housing need.

The research strategy of the project was twofold: firstly, to use data from the OPCS Longitudinal Study (LS)[7] to examine the possibility of the existence of 'hidden homelessness' among Cornish families and, secondly, to carry out a small-scale study of the housing careers and household circumstances of people living in Cornwall, with a particular emphasis on the ways in which people 'resolve' their housing needs. For the second, ethnographic, part of the study, interviews were carried out with a number of 'Cornish' people together with a smaller number of in-migrants to provide some basis for comparison. For the purposes of the study people were considered to be Cornish if they had been born, and lived most of their lives, in Cornwall, if at least one parent had been born in Cornwall and they had lived most of their lives in Cornwall, or if either of these conditions obtained but they had migrated from Cornwall but returned at a later stage. The interview schedule consisted of a list of both specific and general topics and was designed to explore household composition, housing status and history, kinship relationships and cultural characteristics. Help networks related to kinship groups and attitudes towards family support were paid particular attention and because intergenerational differences, support and change were of especial interest and there was a tight time constraint on the study, middle-aged people were specifically targeted for interview, although some older and younger people were included. All but one respondent lived in the St Austell[8] area and a 'snowball' technique was used to recruit respondents. In all, fourteen Cornish people and five in-migrants were successfully interviewed, with the interviews lasting about an hour. In spite of the limitations imposed by the time constraint the two elements of the study yeilded some rich and fascinating data and pointed to the persistence of some important, if small, differences in household structure and kin behaviour between the Cornish and the non-Cornish.

THE ANALYSIS OF LS DATA

The starting point of the study, the analysis of LS data, gave some indication of the possibility of the ways in which Cornish households may, more than is the case elsewhere in England and Wales, be 'absorbing' homelessness.[9] For the demographic analysis those who were enumerated in Cornwall in both the 1971 and 1981 census were defined as 'Cornish'. Initially a comparison was made between the household structures of Cornish families and families living in the rest of England and Wales and 12 [10] household types, based on the Minimum Household Units as conceived by Ermich, Eversley and Overton, were utilised. Data from the OPCS LS[11] were used to compare the household characteristics of those enumerated in Cornwall at both the 1971 and 1981 Census and those who were enumerated outside of Cornwall in both 1971 and 1981.

The percentages of various household types for Cornwall and for the rest of England and Wales are shown in Table 1. While the proportions of people in the twelve household types are similar for both populations there are some small but important differences. In the Cornish sample there is an over-representation of households containing elderly couples, elderly single persons and complex households, and there is a slight over-representation of households comprised of a lone parent with a dependent child and a non-dependent adult.

TABLE 1

Household structure of those enumerated in Cornwall 1971 and 1981 compared with those enumerated outside of Cornwall in both years.

Households 1981	Cornwall %	Not Cornwall %
One person aged less than 65 & over	6.7	5.7
Elderly Couple	12.3	8.5
One person aged less than 65	3.2	3.8
Two or more adults no elderly	3.1	4.5
Couple no dependent children	12.0	13.3
Couple dependent children	25.8	28.3
Couple dependent children + non dependent children + adult	13.5	14.1
Couple with non dependent children, no elderly	9.8	10.8
One parent plus dependent children	1.8	2.0
One parent + dependent children + non dependent children	0.7	0.2
Two or more families	1.1	1.0
Complex household with one or more elderly	9.8	7.5
numbers	**2,573**	**385,001**

Source: OPCS Longitudinal Study

Whilst the higher proportion of elderly single persons and elderly couples in the Cornish population is not surprising given the long term importance of Cornwall as a retirement destination, the larger number of 'complex households' may indicate the existence of 'hidden' or 'absorbed' households. There is also an under-representation of couples both with and without dependent children in the Cornish population. Whilst this could be a function of the higher proportion of elderly-person households, even when age is controlled (Table 2) the difference between the two populations while reduced, is still present. This difference might be accounted for either by imbalances between in- and out-migration or by the absorption of potential households of this type into other household structures. It is also apparent that when controlling on age, households containing one person aged under 65 and those containing two unmarried adults (and no others), are under-represented in the Cornish population. Possibly for similar reasons.

TABLE 2
Household structure of 'non-elderly' households. Those enumerated in Cornwall 1971 and 1981 compared with those enumerated outside of Cornwall in both years.

Households 1981	Cornwall %	Not Cornwall %
One person aged less than 65 & over	3.9	4.5
Two or more adults	3.8	5.3
Couple no dependent children	14.8	12.5
Couple dependent children	31.8	33.0
Couple dependent children + non-dependent children + adult	16.6	16.4
Couple with non-dependent children	12.1	12.5
One parent plus dependent children	2.2	2.3
One parent + dependent children + non-dependent children	0.9	0.3
Two or more families	1.3	1.2
Complex household (elderly excluded)	12.0	8.7
numbers	**2,083**	**330,181**

Source: OPCS Longitudinal Study

The data shown in Tables 1 and 2 thus give a hint of differences in household structure which may indicate 'potential' households hidden within other household structures. The firmest evidence for the existence of hidden potential households in the LS data, however, lies with complex households. While other households may have the potential for division this is not statistically visible; potentially separate households may be more apparent in the complex type. For example, a potentially separate single-person household is more easily seen in a complex household than in one where two generations of the same family are living together. Complex households, too, though they probably represent only some of the hidden-potential households, may evidence other variables which characterise those households with the potential to divide into further, separate households. With this in mind, comparisons were made between, firstly, the characteristics of Cornish complex households and non-complex households and, secondly, Cornish complex households and complex households enumerated outside of Cornwall.

Tables 3, 4, 5 and 6 show comparisons between complex and other households inside and outside Cornwall using a number of variables. It can be seen that differences between the two populations are small, especially when complex households are compared. However, there are some dissimilarities which warrant attention.

TABLE 3

A comparison of the tenure of LS members in complex and non-complex households enumerated in Cornwall 1971 and 1981 with those enumerated outside of Cornwall in both years.

	CORNWALL %		NOT CORNWALL %	
Tenure 1981	All Complex Households	All Other Households	All Complex Households	All Other Households
Owner occupied	68.0	63.0	59.0	62.0
Council	21.0	24.0	30.0	27.0
Private rented	12.0	12.0	10.0	10.0
numbers	**278**	**2,284**	**32,686**	**351,571**

Source: OPCS Longitudinal Study

Table 3 indicates that Cornish complex households are more likely to live in owner-occupied houses, with 68% of the Cornish sample and 59% of the England and Wales sample doing so, and 21% and 30% respectively renting from the council. While these figures may be partly dependent upon the amount of council housing available there is also the possibility that there are other differences between the populations. Table 4, for example, shows that Cornish households generally are more likely to be headed by a person aged over 54. While this is reflective of the larger proportion of older people in the population of Cornwall, there is also a greater tendency for younger people to live in households headed by an older person in the Cornish group than is the case for the rest of England and Wales.

TABLE 4

A comparison of age of heads of households of LS members in complex and non-complex households enumerated in Cornwall 1971 and 1981 with those enumerated outside Cornwall in both years.

	CORNWALL %		NOT CORNWALL %	
Age 1981	All Complex Households	All Other Households	All Complex Households	All Other Households
Under 55	17	58	20	66
55 - 60	14	13	9	12
61 & over	77	29	71	22
numbers	**278**	**2,284**	**32,686**	**351,571**

Source: OPCS Longitudinal Study

Tables 5 and 6 look at households in relationship to the number of wage-earners (5) and marital status (6). Not surprisingly, given the high rates of unemployment, Cornish households in general are less likely to be characterised by having multiple wage-earners, but the experiences of complex households in this respect are almost identical for both populations. There is a difference, however, when marital status is considered. Cornish complex households are more likely to contain people who are separated. This could be indicative of slightly different attitudes towards the resolution of marriage breakdown and could be also hint at a readiness of families to re-incorporate those whose have suffered broken relationships before the break has been legally recognised.

Thus it can be seen that while differences evident in the demographic data are small, some types of household structure are found to be more common in the Cornish population than in the population of the rest of England and

Wales. And while further statistical analyses are needed to explore the data in more depth, the analysis thus far presents some evidence of the presence of family structures and behaviours among the Cornish population which are in some respects different and might have a greater potential to absorb homelessness. The extent of such differences was explored, at least in a preliminary way, in the interviews.

TABLE 5

A comparison of number of wage earners (men aged 16-65, women aged 16-60) in households of LS members in complex and non-complex households enumerated in Cornwall 1971 and 1981 with those enumerated outside Cornwall in both years.

	CORNWALL %		NOT CORNWALL %	
Earners 1981	All Complex Households	All Other Households	All Complex Households	All Other Households
None	25	25	24	17
1 Earner	49	34	50	30
2 Earners	19	29	19	36
3+ Earners	7	12	7	17
numbers	**189**	**1,989**	**24,181**	**301,919**

Source: OPCS Longitudinal Study

AN ETHNOGRAPHIC PILOT STUDY

Social historical accounts of Cornwall are replete with examples of the distinctiveness of Cornish traditions, culture and behaviour. Much of the uniqueness of Cornish life has been seen to relate to the organisation of occupational life around mining, farming and fishing, together with Cornwall's linguistic traditions. Less has been written about family life as such, but there are accounts of extended kin relationships and 'cousin' networks operating not just in Cornwall, but spread out across the continents.[12] These relationships were, at least partially, occupationally related and mining especially had very

TABLE 6
Marital status of LS members in complex and non-complex households
enumerated in Cornwall 1971 and 1981 with those enumerated outside
Cornwall in both years.

	CORNWALL %		NOT CORNWALL %	
Marital Status 1981	All Complex Households	All Other Households	All Complex Households	All Other Households
Single	34.7	17.8	34.0	20.1
First married *	34.3	63.1	34.8	61.7
Remarried	2.6	5.5	3.1	5.8
Divorced	2.6	2.6	4.4	2.8
Widowed	19.9	10.1	20.2	8.0
Separated	5.9	0.9	3.4	1.6
numbers	**271**	**2,029**	**32,006**	**311,354**

* includes cohabitees
Source: OPCS Longitudinal Study

specific organisational characteristics[13]. The decline of mining also helped to precipitate the migration, both temporary and permanent, of Cornish miners and their families and helped to establish world-wide kin networks. The 'wheelbarrow' farming[14] that frequently accompanied mining also had an effect, although of a different kind, upon family relationships. If families had small plots of land to tend, perhaps with animals, then wives and children would have been needed to help. Joint family effort would have been important, just as it is in farming generally. Farming, fishing and mining in most areas were, and often still are, associated with close-knit kin and community ties.[15] The specific traditions of Cornwall were likely to strengthen such networks further. The shared cultural understandings engendered by language also tend to mark peoples out as separate from others and perhaps more dependent upon each other. In spite of the lack of use over several generations of the Cornish language, the shared understandings and expectations about mutual responsibility may persist over a much longer period of time. Certainly a reading of Cornish social history encourages an expectation of cultural and family traditions that might more readily absorb homelessness locally, perhaps as well as, in another way, encouraging out-migration as a possible solution to various types of economic deprivation.

The respondents in the pilot study certainly demonstrated a strong element of family help in resolving housing needs in a variety of ways. Only *one* of the Cornish sample did not report any family help at all. Of the other thirteen respondents, all had lived with parents at some stage, or had their adult children living with them, or been part of joint households of one kind or another. Many of the respondents indicated that shared housing had been a necessity for them, rather than as a result of free choice. Often the sharing was at the beginning of a marriage when a young couple could not afford separate housing and there was no chance of being allocated a council house. Parents, too, frequently helped their children to purchase a house, especially if a shared household had become overcrowded. Thus the majority of the respondents had experienced living in 'complex' households and two of the respondents were currently in such households.

The absorption of homelessness may be beneficial in a number of ways- a young couple may be given a start, care may be provided for an elderly relative, expenditure on housing may be shared - but it is also frequently the case that people would prefer to be separate. Many families share the preference for relatives being 'near but not with'. An example of this from the study is furnished by an owner occupier who was giving accommodation to her brother and his girlfriend. When asked how she felt about sharing she replied, 'It would be nice to have our first home to ourselves really. . . my husband's not, basically not too keen on them either. It's not that they don't get on, but I think he'd basically like to come home to his own house. . . They're there all the time. I think he's getting fed up with my family. You can't blame him really'. The financial circumstances of the respondent's brother and his girlfriend made it extremely unlikely that they would be able to afford separate housing in the near future. Thus necessity was often the spur to sharing. It was also found that where an elderly person was present in the household of the respondent this was often the result of the housing need of the younger resident(s) rather than because the elderly person needed care. The needs of the younger members of Cornish families, at least in the survey group, would appear to be the most pressing.

Whatever the reasons for sharing, then, sample members had 'normally' experienced shared housing with other family members, usually precipitated by the needs of younger family members who were unable to afford separate housing and who felt they would be, or had actually been, unsuccessful in renting from the council.

The lack of availability of council housing was a factor in the decision of some respondents to resolve their housing need by buying poor quality housing. One respondent who had bought a house without basic amenities and had initially been very unhappy with her circumstances, reported that they had bought the house because they had been 'desperate for somewhere to live'. The sample actually only contained one person who had ever lived in a council house - probably the result of the 'snowball' recruitment. However, respondents who would have liked council accommodation had either been informed, or assumed, that because of its general lack of availability they would be unlikely to be successful in obtaining it.

There was also a great deal of evidence of shared ownership through inheritance and of relatives buying houses as a joint enterprise or buying from other family members. Some of the mechanics of shared ownership through inheritance are quite complicated; for example, one respondent effectively owned five-eighths of the house that she was living in . A proportion derived from sales within the family and of part of the house being left in trust for her siblings on the death of her maternal aunt. Shared ownership and inheritance also occasionally derived through the practice of self-build. Two of the respondents, for example, were living in a house that belonged to the wife's mother, whose step-father had built it together with other houses on the same site at the turn of the century. Another couple had built their own house on some land given to them by the wife's father; the husband had previously helped both his sisters to 'build their own', again on the same settlement. Yet another respondent had been involved in self-build in order to obtain a house large enough to accommodate her mother as well as her own immediate family.

Other respondents had joined together with other family members in order to be able to afford to buy. One respondent's mother had sold her own house to help to finance a deal and another reported that her maternal uncle, his wife and children had bought a house together with the uncle's parents. Thus, often for financial reasons, but also, especially in the case of self-build, because it is traditional practice, family members had cooperated to obtain housing as groups, give each other financial assistance and generally provided resolutions to pressing housing need.

Family networks were also important in locating housing. Only six of the fourteen respondents had met their housing needs through the open market (one of these by self-build). Seven had obtained their present housing directly through a relative. Many of the respondents also reported a variety of ways in which relatives had helped each other with housing and in other ways. Kinship assistance for the respondents, indeed, whilst it was most common in the immediate family, extended far beyond help with housing. Finch and Mason[16] in Greater Manchester found among their respondents that there was a general agreement that families should help each other in 'deserving cases' and when the assistance needed was fairly limited. Obviously it is difficult to quantify what is meant by 'deserving' cases and 'limited' assistance but certainly among the Cornish respondents the help given was frequently extensive: for example, a £10,000 loan to buy a house, moving elderly relatives to live next door in order to provide the level of help felt to be necessary. It is interesting that Finch and Mason felt that the assistance given to family members was greatest among families with 'an extensive history of mutual aid'. Perhaps this idea of a history of aid provides us with at least one reason for the seemingly greater level and intensity of help among the Cornish respondents. The more extensive family and kin networking suggested in historical accounts of Cornish life may have had a long term effect upon present behaviour.

As only five in-migrants were interviewed it is difficult and possibly dangerous to make too many comparisons. However, among the migrants all had been owner-occupiers prior to moving to Cornwall and all had benefited from the relatively lower house prices in Cornwall, being able to make considerable gains from the difference between their selling and purchase prices. One couple had managed to start a business with the surplus and others had managed to buy larger houses. Unlike the Cornish sample, none had bought sub-standard housing out of necessity, although two had done so because they had wanted properties to renovate. While close family ties were apparent and one couple reported family help with house purchase, there was no evidence of families solving housing problems by absorbing other members into joint households. However, this latter may have been a function of the small numbers in the group and generalisations are unsafe.

CONCLUSION

While the study was undertaken largely to set the parameters for a larger scale study on Cornish housing, the data obtained in themselves give some insights into the ways in which Cornish families assist their members in the resolution of housing need. The information collected in such a small-scale study is necessarily inconclusive and has suggested further research questions rather than providing definitive answers. However, both the statistical analysis of the LS data and the ethnographic data contain strong suggestions that the actions of family members are indeed helping to absorb potential homelessness. Indeed, it would appear that family activity is operating as one of the 'crisis minimising' factors in Cornish housing.

REFERENCES

1. For further discussion see: Andrew George, *Homes For Locals in Cornwall / Chyow rag Genesygyon yn Kernow* , Truro, 1990. Bernard Deacon, Andrew George, Ronald Perry, *Cornwall at the Crossroads?*, Redruth, 1988. Joy Lennon, *The Homeless in Cornwall,*, Truro, 1991

2. See: Christine Lambert, Syd Jeffers, Paul Burton & Glen Bramley, *Homelessness in Rural Areas*, Salisbury, 1992.

3. This is based upon DoE Local Housing returns. Some caution must be exercised in using these fugures to estimate homelessness. Firstly councils do not collect statistics in a uniform way and secondly the definitions of homelesness under the 1977 and later Housing Acts are very restrictive. In effect they ammount to 'rooflessness' and consequently exclude many in dire housing need. Nevertheless given the economic disparity between Cornwall and South West England one would have expected the numbers of 'roofless' in Cornwall to be much higher.

4. Malcolm Williams, *Housing the Cornish* in Philip Payton (ed.), *Cornwall Since the War*, Redruth, forthcoming 1993.

5. Lambert *et al.*, 1992.

6. Mary Buck, Lyn Bryant, Malcolm Williams, *Housing and Households in Cornwall: A Pilot Study of Cornish Families*, Plymouth, 1993. This report which gives a full account of the research findings is available from the Faculty of Human Sciences, University of Plymouth.

7. The OPCS Longitudinal Study is a set of records of various events relating to 1% of the population of England and Wales (and Cornwall) - about 500,000 people. These can be linked in various ways for analysis. Initially all people born on each of four dates each year were selected from the 1971 Census. From 1971, as new births occur on these four dates and as immigrants with these birth dates register with the NHS these people join the LS. Further samples of those with the LS birth dates were taken in the 1981and 1991 Censuses. Thus the LS represents a continuous sample of the population, rather than a sample taken at any one point. LS data from the 1991 Census will be available at the end of 1993.

8. St Austell was chosen for the site of the study as it both retains some of its industrial character and being at a little distance from the coast it has been less affected by tourism than many towns and is, indeed, seen by many people as a very Cornish town.

9. 'Hidden homelessness' is difficult to locate, partly because the term has been used in a number of different ways and it is also a subjective as well as an objective state. For example one young adult living with parents may have no desire to leave the parental home, while another may be extremely anxious to set up in a separate household. We have tended in this paper to talk about 'absorbing' or 'absorbed' homelessness as this better describes the idea that some household structures are better able than others to absorb potentially separate households.

10. A 12 household categorisation developed from Minimal Household Units has been used in other research (for example, Malcolm Williams and Angela Dale, *Measuring Housing Deprivation Using the OPCS Longitudinal Study LS Working Paper 72*, London, 1991. In this paper where complex households are compared with other types, 'two plus' families are collapsed into 'complex Households' (see Tables 2 and 3).

11. The LS is the only unclustered data source that will allow longitudinal comparisons between Cornwall and England and Wales. Though raw census data would allow a comparison between the 1981 population of Cornwall with that of England and Wales only a longitudinal sample can distinguish those who had been present at the previous census. This is important because there are significant differences between the long term population of Cornwall and those people that moved to Cornwall between 1971 and 1981, with the latter often more closely resembling the characteristics of LS members in England and Wales (see Williams, 1993).

12. There are numerous accounts of the support offered to Cornish miners and their families travelling abroad and many Cornish families continue to correspond with cousins who they have never seen.

13. Philip Payton, *The Making of Modern Cornwall: Historical Experience and the Persistence of "Difference"* , Redruth, 1992.

14. Ibid.

15. There are numerous studies of communities in Britain which describe the traditional networks in farming and coal mining areas. For a collection of studies see Ronald Frankenberg, *Communities in Britain*, Harmondsworth, 1969.

16. Janet Finch and Jennifer Mason, *Negotiating Family Responsibility*, London, 1993.

'BE FOREVER CORNISH!'
SOME OBSERVATIONS ON THE ETHNOREGIONAL MOVEMENT IN CONTEMPORARY CORNWALL
Caroline Vink

INTRODUCTION

'Come to the delectable Duchy' is a slogan that has attracted tourists from far and near to Cornwall to spend their holidays. Charmed by the warm weather, hidden coves and misty moors they have flocked in great numbers to the small peninsula in the south-west of Britain. Many have come across the pixies and pasties and the stories of King Arthur and have been amazed at the 'romantic' 'differentness' of Cornwall. Yet very few have noticed that in Cornwall there is a deeper feeling of 'difference'. This sentiment is expressed in terms other than the 'guide-book' image presented to tourists. Indeed, this century has seen the revival of Cornish identity and culture and has witnessed the emergence of an ethnoregional movement, developments similar to those in other regions of Europe.

The Cornish ethnoregional movement is rooted in the 'discovery' of the Celtic origins of Cornwall at the beginning of this century. Interest in these Celtic roots led to perhaps the most striking aspect of Cornish ethnoregionalism: the revival of the Cornish language. Cornish, a Celtic language related to Breton and Welsh, started its retreat when Cornwall was joined with England during the tenth century and finally disappeared as a spoken language in the eighteenth century. The cautious attempts to reinstall the language and to revive the Celtic roots has catalysed feelings of 'difference' and enhanced awareness of a Cornish identity. After World War II this led to the rise of a more political movement, with organisations calling for an autonomous Cornwall. The persistently appalling state of the Cornish economy has been a continuous source of inspiration for this political movement.

There has been relatively little attention paid to the developments in Cornwall, despite the interest in ethnoregional movements elsewhere in

Europe. Those academics who have addressed the 'Cornish question' have been historians or political scientists, with little work undertaken by ethnographers or anthropologists.[1] To many Cornwall is a confusing case. Although there are signs of a persisting 'difference', the vindicating roots for this 'difference' are very concealed. The ethnoregional movement in itself is very small, with only a limited core of activists. Compared to the more established claims of Wales and Scotland, the Cornish claims are hardly taken seriously by the British government. Despite a limited popular awareness of a constitutional identity lent by the Duchy, Cornwall does not have any special status in Britain. It is ostensibly an English county and the British government has rejected all requests to recognise Cornwall as being anything other than an administrative entity. This has led to a duality where most people - certainly outside Cornwall - see Cornwall as an ordinary English county, while the activists of the Cornish movement and their sympathizers claim a very different status. What makes Cornwall interesting is not so much the question of whether the ethnic roots claimed by the activists are genuine, but that there has been an emergence of an ethnoregional movement at all.

In this article, which is based partly on a doctoral thesis presented at the University of Amsterdam, specific insights into the motivations and experiences of the Cornish movement in particular (and thus ethnoregional movements in general) are sought. Three separate events are singled-out for comment: the spelling debate, the 1992 general election, and the Cornish petition to the European Parliament. Research into these issues was carried out in fieldwork among the leaders and representatives of the Cornish movement during the first months of 1992.

In the process of ethnoregionalisation there are two elements which are important in understanding the phenomenon: the role of ethnicity and the desire to re-invigorate the region. The definition of ethnoregional movements adopted here is that proposed by Hechter.[2] He distinguishes ethnoregional movements from other kinds of regional movements (whose demands are couched solely in terms of material demands) by arguing that the salience of ethnic unrest is rooted in a perceived inequality between the region and the state in which symbols of 'difference' are 'revived' or even 'invented' to articulate regional grievances. In time, the promotion of 'difference' becomes an end in itself and thus the ethnic dimension of the movement is reinforced.

In this process an increasing awareness of ethnic identity and distinguishing cultural markers gains importance and becomes the base for regional claims. It underlines the concept of 'difference', and newly-emergent cultural organisations play a key role in bringing like-minded people together. Although the ethnic base of some of the organisations within the Cornish movement might be debatable, their emergence evinces this process nature of ethnicity. In general, it is appropriate to describe the Cornish movement as ethnoregional. Its activities are often directed at the apalling socio-economic state of the region, but the inspiration comes from a common belief in the uniqueness of Cornwall and its distinctive past.

THE EMERGENCE OF THE MOVEMENT

The growth of the Cornish movement has been a gradual adoption by a relatively small group of people of the idea that Cornwall is 'different' and 'worth fighting for'. This emergence was not a sudden reaction, but was a process that had started at the beginning of this century. Interest in the separate culture and identity of Cornwall originated in a wider interest in the ancient Celtic roots of Britain and Ireland, which emerged at the end of the last century. Inspired by the wider 'Celtic Revival' movement, enthusiasm for Cornwall's Celtic past led to a determined revival of the Cornish language and to an increase in Celtic-Cornish cultural activities, such as music and dance, and even the creation of a Cornish Gorsedd.

Parallel to this developing interest in Celtic culture there was the deteriorating state of the Cornish socio-economic situation. As a remote periphery of Britain, Cornwall was never a very prosperous area, except for a brief spell during the late eighteenth and early nineteenth centuries. But the collapse of mining in the later nineteenth century made the economic situation much worse. Many people were forced to leave Cornwall to look for a better living. Midway through the twentieth century this migration trend was reversed when people from other parts of Britain started to settle in Cornwall, looking for a better and healthier place to live. Many Cornish people perceived this change as a threat. The newcomers - often better educated - took the better jobs and bought the better houses. Resentments and perception of inequality arose among the indigenous Cornish population. Within the small group of 'Cornish culture enthusiasts' it also led to changes in perception. Meeting their 'fellow Celts' and other European minorities at cultural conferences and learning of their struggles outside the cultural field, encouraged the Cornish to resort to political action. A few years after World War II the first real political organisation, Mebyon Kernow, was created, its political agenda consisting entirely of Cornish issues. Subsequently, other political and pressure group organisations emerged, each aiming to protect Cornwall and the Cornish against the alleged deleterious effects of rapid socio-economic changes.

The emerging Cornish ethnoregional movement has won little attention from the British government, despite its patchy but measurable impact within Cornwall itself. On the national level, Cornwall has been treated increasingly as part of the wider south-west region when it comes to issues like regional planning, and most of the protest generated by the Cornish movement has been simply ignored. Some of the organisations have been succesful in mobilizing support on specific issues (for example, the Euro-constituency campaign), but none of the issues has led to sustained mass support. The credibility of the Cornish movement has not been helped by its many internal disputes. From close quarters, the history of the Cornish movement seems to be one of continuous fissions and newly emergent organisations. But this is typical of the formative phases in the history of ethnoregional movements generally, as Esman has noted:

As ethnoregional movements expand and draw support from
more diversified sources, the leaders of the movement who agree
on the ultimate goals of independence or autonomy may begin to
differ over appropriate intermediate goals, tactics, and timing,
since they must decide whether to use violence or peaceful
electoral politics, and whether to place an emphasis on cultural,
economic, or political issues.[3]

There is hardly a common ideology that characterises the Cornish
movement. The simple concept that ties the various activists together is the
shared perception that their homeland is under attack. When it comes to
deciding on a strategy to improve the situation they are utterly divided on the
methods, and even on the nature of Cornish 'difference'. The factionalism that
has characterised the spelling debate within the language arm of the Cornish
movement gives some excellent examples of internal differences among the
activists. But equally, the events of the 1992 general election demonstrate the
threat to which ethnoregional movements become vulnerable at a certain stage
of their development, a threat recognised by Esman in his comparative study
of ethnoregional movements: 'Competition from established political groups
who find it expedient to embrace some ethnically based symbols and demands
in order to neutralize the appeal of ethnoregional movements and to co-opt parts
of these movements' growing constituencies'.[4] The Cornish petition to the
European Parliament is illustrative of yet another example of developments
within the ethnoregional movements in Europe: the embracing of the idea of
European unification as a potential solution to the problems of the ethnoregions
in Europe. Thus the fieldwork which underpins this article identified three
elements within the Cornish movement which are in fact exemplars of the wider
experience of ethnoregional movements in Western Europe: the propensity for
internal dissension, the vulnerability to co-option by established political
parties, and the appeal to a 'Europe of the regions'.

THE SPELLING DEBATE

Tim Saunders, a Cornish activist, must have been struck by a moment of
prophecy when he wrote in 1983:

> The revival of Cornish (language) seems to be reaching the end
> of one of its periodic cycles - but with the difference that Cornish
> activity now takes place outside the Gorsedd and Old Cornwall
> contexts. There is a chance of continuity until the next upsurge.
> Indeed, a wider public awareness allows for a qualitative change
> in the character of Cornish activity. The next ten years promise
> interest and excitement.[5]

And interest and excitement there were among the Cornish language organisations. As every language is two things - a medium of communication and a symbol of the identity for the community of its users[6] - the Cornish language is a confusing phenomenon. Being a revived language, it is obviously not a medium for communication among the Cornish population, apart from the few who have become fluent in it. It has, however, become a strong symbol for the Cornish movement and the activists involved, even for those who have never bothered to learn the language. The mere existence of a separate language underlines the distinctiveness of Cornwall and, therefore, legitimises the efforts of the activists. As DeVos writes, 'ethnicity is frequently related more to the symbol of a separate language than to its actual use by all members of the group'.[7]

Thus the emotional upsurge within the language movement when the spelling reform proposal by Ken George was adopted by the Cornish Language Board in 1987 was not completely unexpected. The revival was still in a vulnerable stage, and the group able to converse in Cornish at anything like a sustained or sophiscated level was still rather small. The revival itself had undergone many attacks from outside, especially from academic circles. And within Cornwall there was a strong resentment, a belief that any attempt at spelling reform at this stage was bound to cause division and confusion. But although the spelling debate was to a great extent an emotional controversy amongst the users, it also exposed the deeper problems of the entire Cornish movement.

It was to be expected that spelling reform would be attempted at some stage of the revival, criticism of the revived 'Unified' spelling having come from both Ken George and Richard Gendall, the latter proposing a 'Traditional' or 'Modern' spelling based on Late Cornish. The adoption of George's 'Phonemic' spelling by the Cornish Language Board in 1987 caused an enormous schism and for some years the revival was paralysed by the differences in opinion. The problems were initially fought out on the personal, emotional level. People used public meetings to denounce each other's spelling and took every opportunity to ridicule the other side. Some 'Unified' supporters accused the 'Phonemic' spelling of being a made-up 'computer Cornish', purely academic, without real Cornish roots. Other, 'Phonemic' supporters pictured the 'Unified' adherents as dinosaurs, unable to make adjustments to modern demands. 'Modern' speakers claimed that they were merely picking-up Cornish where it had left off, without recourse to invention and revision. After the emotional attacks, the academic debate began. But unable to resolve their differences, the three groups retreated to their three camps: the Cornish Language Board ('Phonemic', but with a half-hearted accommodation of 'Unified'), the Cornish Language Council ('Modern'), and Agan Tavas ('Unified'). Many who were not directly involved in the language debate tried to mediate in the conflict by stressing the potentially disastrous effects on the state of the revival and the danger of putting-off prospective learners:

The obvious danger that should be avoided at all costs is that the

man in the Cornish street will say (and I won't attempt to imitate
Cornish dialect!) 'Well, I always thought learning Cornish was
daft, and now they can't even make up their minds how to spell
it!'[8]

During the fieldwork period most of the spelling debate seemed to be
over, particularly the hitherto frequent personal attacks. The controversy
among the various organisations had crystallised, the organisations convinced
of their own goals and strengthening their causes by organising language classes
and promoting publications. In interviews with the representatives of the three
'sides' much bitterness and resentment remained among those directly involved,
but it had not made them retire from the scene. The people supporting
'Phonemic' Cornish seemed to be those most sure of what they were doing and
were single-minded in their determination that their version of the language
would triumph. The opinion of many 'Phonemic' supporters was that the
'Unified' and 'Modern' supporters were marginalized groups. One
'Phonemic' supporter said this:

> The people involved in the 'Unified' spelling have not been really
> involved in the debate. They don't use the spoken language, they
> only talk about Cornish in English. They belong to an older
> generation. The 'Late ("Modern") Cornish' believers have the
> wrong starting point. They are backward looking and romanticise
> the Cornish past. They are so marginalized and want to start
> something all over again. They have generally not worked with
> the Cornish movement.[9]

'Unified' followers demonstrated profound emotional commitment to
the language. Several of them had been among the 'pioneer' language learners,
and found themselves having to defend their now 'threatened' pathfinding work
in the Revival. A few of them had even learned Cornish from Morton Nance
himself. Their main argument was 'why throw away sixty years of work, it
would be the death of Cornish once more!'.[10]

The controversy between 'Unified' and 'Phonemic' was in
several respects a generational conflict. To the older generation - involved
during the pioneer stages of learning the language - the language was a symbol,
they had to fight for it. The younger generation - who started learning the
language at a time when it was becoming generally accepted that there was a
revival of Cornish, albeit on a small scale - saw the new spelling as a way
forward. The arguments used by the 'Modern' followers were of a different
nature. Arguing that their form of the language was based on Cornish as it was
last spoken, they insisted that their spelling reflected an authentic Cornish
culture. In their eyes the other spellings were part of the made-up 'kilt and
tartan' pseudo-culture they resisted, with the 'invented' and 'hypothetical'
form of 'Phonemic' being in fact a greater travesty than the older 'Unified'.

Activists in the wider Cornish movement, those not involved directly in the language revival, had wisely tried to stay out of the dispute. Although many shared the opinion that, 'if there is an argument, the language is alive!',[11] in fact the language debate had revealed the impotence of the entire Cornish movement and its inability to develop common future strategies. Reflecting the confusion of the language debate, the wider Cornish movement had been unable to construct a co-ordinated ideological view of the future, or even to agree priorities and tactics. Given this uncertainty, the way was wide open for the established political parties to co-opt the symbolism and rhetoric of the Cornish movement.

THE 1992 GENERAL ELECTION

The general election that took place at the end of the fieldwork period, raised hopes of change. Many saw this election as a possibility to reverse the downward socio-economic trend in Cornwall. The 'coming election' came up in many interviews with representatives of the movement. Without exception, they hoped for a change in power (up to then the Tories had four out of the five MPs for Cornwall), believing Cornwall would benefit from such a change. Someone voiced this feeling by writing 'if Cornwall does not use this election to send its Tory MPs packing back across the Tamar, the country's long decline will continue and probably accelerate'.[12] The belief in a possible change was intensified through the upsurge in the devolution debate in Scotland. The media paid much attention to this debate, even addressing the issue of whether Scotland could become a member of the European Community. The debate prompted discussions in Cornish newspapers on home-rule and the territorial integrity for Cornwall, raising the hopes of Cornish activists.

The role of the Cornish movement in this election proved rather ambiguous. It became clear at an early stage of the campaign that neither Mebyon Kernow nor the Cornish Nationalist Party would be contesting any seats. Although ostensibly reflecting a lack of funding, this failure in reality demonstrated that both parties had not devised a sound and coherent political programme that might appeal to the electorate. The lack of political vision and a credible alternative had been plaguing both parties for some time. CNP had never been able to command much electoral support. MK, on the other hand, had been relatively successful in elections at the local and European levels, but had never achieved credible results in general elections. Indeed, MK's attitude towards the coming election was one of resignation, an MK press statement admitting sadly that, 'We must recognize that under the present electoral system, people will often vote for the "mainstream" candidate least offensive to them and it is difficult to persuade people, however sympathetic, to vote for a party perceived to have little chance, such as Mebyon Kernow'.[13]

The established parties, however, had become increasingly successful in winning votes on the 'Cornish ticket'. Many MPs in Cornwall had been sympathetic to Cornish issues and some of them had even joined MK when it was still in its 'pressure group' stage. But other MPs - according to activists in the movement - were completely ignorant of Cornish issues (they referred 'mainly to Tory MPs), or at least did not understand the specific problems of unemployment, housing and environment in Cornwall. And yet the 1992 general election was for Cornwall a kind of a historical marker, because each of the candidates in Cornish constituencies had Cornish issues on the top of their agendas. Without exception - although the intensity fluctuated - the established parties embraced the traditional issues voiced by the Cornish movement. They called for action on the disastrous state of the Cornish economy, housing, unemployment and education. Most candidates boasted their Cornish descent or connections, and presented themselves as 'true Cornishmen'. The Liberal Democrats were especially adept at putting Cornish issues on their political agenda (Cornwall has a high proportion of Lib Dem voters compared to the national level). One of their candidates was a well-known activist in the Cornish movement and others were clearly sympathetic towards the movement.

However, the opinions of the activists within the movement were divided. Some welcomed the change in attitude of the established parties, seeing it as the ultimate victory of the movement in having put Cornish issues on a wider political agenda - forcing the 'establishment' to take Cornwall seriously. Others were more sceptical about this apparent upsurge of interest in Cornwall in the established parties. They were not only afraid that this might mean the end of the movement's own direct political influence, but also saw the situation as a temporary flirtation in order to win votes. One older activist voiced these feelings by saying:

> Well, you know, according to me, attention to Cornish issues is of great importance to Cornish voters. But I actually rather doubt the sincerity of some of the official party candidates. I wonder whether they will be able to stand up against their mother party when matters come to a head. Personality is of utmost importance to a Cornish voter. It does not work when they get someone from Devon to put up in a Cornish seat.[14]

MK did attempt to stay involved in the election. Although it did not have a candidate, it intended to publish voting recommendations, supporting candidates who would be prepared to put Cornish issues first. In order to give such a recommendation it sent a questionnaire to all candidates standing in Cornwall, seeking their view on matters of importance to Cornwall. They wanted opinions on matters traditionally voiced by MK: Cornish integrity, identity and culture (issues like recognising the Cornish as an ethnic group, the right of the Cornish to decide their own future through a Cornish assembly, establishing Cornwall as a region, a Cornish Development Agency), employment (issues such as positive discrimination in favour of the Cornish), housing (restrictions on in-migration and the sale of council houses; second and holiday homes), and education (calling for an university for Cornwall). Most questions were stated very vaguely, the candidates were left five options, ranging from 'strongly agree' to 'strongly disagree'. Replies were received from half of the candidates. The reactions to the questionnaire were divided, although on some issues a consensus was reached. The candidates agreed on issues like a university for Cornwall, the need for a Cornish Development Agency, and the demand for affordable homes for the Cornish. There was support for the idea that 'the only region for Cornwall is Cornwall'. The opinions differed enormously when it came to restrictions on migration, second and holiday homes, and the sale of council houses. It is doubtful whether the questionnaire threw any light on the real opinions of the candidates, since the questions were rather vague and no commitment was sought from the respondents. In the end MK did not recommend any candidate in particular but wrote that:

> The voters of Cornwall should question their candidate closely to determine whether knowledge and understanding of Cornish issues is real or merely superficial electioneering. We recognize that no particular candidate or party is totally prepared to put Cornwall first and our advice is to vote for the candidate best able to defeat candidates who somehow show no understanding or sympathy for the problems of Cornwall.[15]

With hopes so high, the actual results of the election caused considerable disappointment among the Cornish movement. On the national level, the Tories had kept their overall majority and in Cornwall the Tories kept three out of five seats, the others won by Liberal Democrats. Activists in the movement felt that the election results extinguished the hope that had arisen before the election, especially since the home-rule dream for Scotland now had also vanished. One observer expressed the general feeling by writing, 'we as a Cornish nation have just been sentenced to five more years of unemployment, lower wages and total disregard for Cornwall and the Cornish people'.[16]

Time will tell whether this election was significant in the short history of Cornish ethnoregionalism. It may be that the political parties (MK and CNP) representing the movement have lost all credibility. And yet, the Cornish issues the movement has been fighting for have moved to the forefront of the Cornish political agenda. The situation in Cornwall seems to correspond to a great extent to that described by Esman,[17] where established parties have been successful in taking away the 'ethnic vote'. The question remains whether the movement, which appears to be adrift at present, will overcome its internal problems and make a major contribution to the debate that will attend the consideration of local government reform in Cornwall. According to one view, 'Mebyon Kernow is committed to doing everything it can to defend government in Cornwall for Cornwall'.[18]

THE PETITION TO THE EUROPEAN PARLIAMENT

From a very early stage the various organisations that comprise the Cornish movement have looked outside Cornwall for support. Initially, support was sought from fellow Celts within the circle of the Celtic nations. But support was also sought from other European minority groups. The idea of European integration has been warmly embraced by both MK and CNP. The political future of Cornwall has been redefined by both parties as 'a regional status for Cornwall within an united Europe'. Underlying reasons for this international outlook were explained by one activist: 'The European links were established at an early stage because London is so ignorant of the whole situation. Europe is a dimension that gives a positive outlook'.[19] The campaign to create a Cornwall-only constituency for the European elections had also emerged from the belief that Cornwall should be recognised as a distinct entity within Europe. CoBER, the Cornish Bureau for European Relations (probably the only body directly promoting European affairs without being funded by the European Commission or Council of Europe), was established in 1987 and has acted as a lobby for Cornwall within the European institutions. Specifically, the lobby was aimed at presenting a petition to the European Parliament, in support of Cornwall's heritage and culture. This petition was initiated by CoBER, in association with the Member of the European Parliament for Cornwall and Plymouth, asking the European Parliament:

> - to examine the dangers now being posed to Cornwall's identity and heritage as - in common with those of other historic European regions - they are subjected to many pressures contained in contemporary social and economic development.

> - within Cornwall these dangers have become acute, with profound implications for Cornish people and their way of life. CoBER therefore requests that a case study should be commissioned, to examine the Cornish situation against the wider background of cultural erosion elsewhere in Europe.[20]

The petition was supported by the various organisations of the Cornish movement, together with the County, District and several Parish councils. Although yet to persuade the Parliament that Cornwall should be treated as a European case-study, CoBER was succesful in building a network of links with sympathetic MEPs, as well as establishing contacts with the European Commision and influencing the Parliament's *Laroni* and draft *Killillea* reports on European cultural issues. In common with other European ethnoregional movements, this activity was seen as one way of by-passing a generally unsympathetic central government at state level and ensuring a place in the emerging European regional debate. From this perspective, the various organisations of the Cornish movement saw the work of CoBER as being of great importance, of winning for Cornwall that place on the European regional agenda.

CONCLUDING REMARKS

The case of Cornwall underlines the importance of perceived inequality between region and state in precipitating the emergence of ethnoregional movements. 'Invented tradition' is employed to enhance the claims of ethnic distinctiveness, and in time elements of that tradition (for example, language revival) are defended by activists as central and legitimate aspects of identity. Certainly, 'being Cornish' has become a plausible alternative to other sources of identity. A wider 'persistence of difference' in modern Cornwall has also lent credibility to the ethnoregional movement. However, the Cornish movement, in a manner typical of Western European ethnoregional movements, has experienced a tendency towards fragmentation and internal dispute (of which the spelling debate is a prime example), while many of its policies have been co-opted by the mainstream 'establishment' parties. And yet, again like other European movements, the Cornish activists have been successful in penetrating the European regional debate. An assertive pride in Cornish cultural activities has emerged (especially in Rugby Football) and there also seems to be a more emancipated Cornish political environment. The question remains, how succesful will be the Cornish ethnoregional movement in the future? Will this small band of activists be able to increase its support, or will its efforts be dissipated through the years? Time will tell, but until then the small group of activists - even against the odds - will go on being Cornish 'bys vykken' (for ever).

REFERENCES

1. The only exception is Mary McArthur, 'The Cornish: A Case Study in Ethnicity', unpublished MSc thesis, University of Bristol, 1988.
2. Michael Hechter and Margaret Levi, 'The comarative analysis of ethnoregional movements', *Ethnic and Racial Studies*, Vol 2, No 3, July 1979.
3. Milton J. Esman, 'Perspectives on ethnic conflict in industrialized societes', in *Ethnic Conflict in the Western World*, London, 1977, p. 377.
4. Esman, 1977, p. 377.
5. Tim Saunders, 'Cornish - symbol and substance', in Cathal O'Lain (ed.), *For A Celtic Future*, Dublin, 1983, p. 258.
6. Sauders, 1983, p. 253.
7. George A. De Vos, *Ethnic Identity, Conflict and Accommodation*, Chicago, 1975, p. 15.
8. Interview with Cornish activist (a), Cornwall, 1992.
9. Interview with Language activist (a), Cornwall, 1992.
10. Interview with Language activist (b), Cornwall, 1992.
11. This view was advanced by Philip Payton during an interview at the Institute of Cornish Studies, 1992.
12. *Western Morning News*, 6 April 1992.
13. Mebyon Kernow Press Statement, 1992.
14. Interview with Cornish activist (b), Cornwall, 1992.
15. Mebyon Kernow Press Statement, 1992.
16. *Western Morning News*, 13 April 1992.
17. Esman, 1977, p. 377.
18. Mebyon Kernow Press Statement, 1992.
19. Interview with Cornish activist (c), Cornwall, 1992.
20. Cornish Bureau for European Relations, *Petition to the European Parliament in support of Cornwall's heritage and culture*, 1988.

THE ACARINE FAUNA OF THE ISLES OF SCILLY

Keith H. Hyatt

SYNOPSIS

This paper lists 169 species of Acari (mites and ticks) from the Isles of Scilly, and of these 56 are recorded for the first time. Identifications to genus or family only of a further 42 taxa which are included in the text are not included in these totals even though the species in question may not be conspecific with closely-related named taxa. Six species, *Pachylaelaps denticulatus* Hirschmann & Krauss (1965), *Gymolaelaps austriaca* Sellnick (1935), *Discourella franzi* Hirschmann & Zirngiebl-Nicol (1969), *Uroobovella appendiculata* Berlese (1910), *Uropoda vulgaris* Hirschmann & Zirngiebl-Nicol (1969), and *Uropoda willmanni* Hirschmann & Zirngiebl-Nicol (1969), all Mesostigmata, are new records for the British Isles.

The bulk of material examined was collected by the author, whilst recent records have been made by Pugh and King (1988), Pugh (1988) and Luxton (1990). Earlier published records from a variety of sources, together with scattered, named material in the collections of the British Museum (Natural History), are included.

INTRODUCTION
GENERAL

The Isles of Scilly lie some 28 miles (45 km) WSW of Land's End. They are an extension of the line of granite bosses which start in the east with Dartmoor and decrease in height towards the west through Bodmin Moor, Hensbarrow Downs, Wendron Moor and Penwith. There are five inhabited islands, St Mary's, Tresco, St Martin's, St Agnes and Bryher. The largest of these, St Mary's, is about two and a quarter miles long and has an area of 1,554 acres (628 hectares). About 40 smaller islands carry vegetation and all are now uninhabited. In addition there are about 150 named rocks which are too exposed or too small to form habitats for vascular plants. In fact many are totally submerged at ordinary high water.

The granite of Scilly is whiter, more sparkling and softer than that of Land's End and this has resulted in peculiarities of the flora being related to the soils to which it gives rise (Lousley 1971). In many places, especially on Peninnis Head , St Mary's and on the south-west side of St Agnes, the granite has been weathered into rocks of most grotesque shapes. The soil is of two main types: 'Head' or 'Rab' is an accumulation of fragments of granite in an advanced state of decomposition, and extensive deposits provide a habitat for the deeper-rooted plants, especially bracken, whilst Blown Sand, containing much white felspar which imparts the characteristic colour, represents a further stage in the disintegration of the granite and Head, and is present in vast accumulations, often high on the islands. Sandy beaches and rocky coves abound. In the north-west part of Bryher, where one inlet is known as Hell Bay, are high granite cliffs which take the full force of the Atlantic gales.

Covean, a sandy and rocky St Agnes bay at low tide

The islands are part of the possessions of the Duchy of Cornwall, whilst they are administered by an all-purpose authority, the Council of the Isles of Scilly, and are not part of Cornwall county, although there is collaboration with Cornwall over certain matters. The Isles of Scilly are part of Watsonian Vice-County 1, West Cornwall. For purposes of recording plant distribution they are designated V.C. 1a by Lousley (1971) and the Cornish Biological Records Unit at the Institute of Cornish Studies, although the Botanical Society of the British Isles refers to them as 1b.

To the British naturalist the Isles of Scilly are unique. The equable nature of their climate permits species of plants from warmer regions than our own to flourish, and it was with this in mind that Augustus Smith, who in 1834 took up his appointment as first Lord Proprietor of the Islands on behalf of the Duchy of Cornwall, founded the world-famous Tresco Abbey Gardens. The islands are also famous for their flowers, especially the early daffodils, grown for the Christmas markets. Normally frosts and snow do not occur on Scilly, but in early 1987 the islands were subjected to a foot of snow and freezing conditions. On all the inhabited islands many trees, shrubs and succulent plants, as well as a large proportion of the evergreen hedges, especially the New Zealand *Pittosporum crassifolium*, forming the windbreaks around the bulb-fields, were killed. The 'giant' tree *Echium*, which had for decades been a feature of Lower Town, St Agnes, was killed by this spell of intense cold. The average rainfall (32.71 in, 830 mm) is slightly less than nearby Cornwall whilst almost identical with that of Britain as a whole, and although there is an abundance of fog at times, there is also plenty of sunshine. In popular literature the islands are known by titles such as 'The Sunshine Isles', 'The Fortunate Isles' and 'The Isles of Flowers'. For an introduction to the history and geography and a first-class account of the flora of the islands, the reader is referred to Lousley (1971) and to later, regularly-updated information at the Isles of Scilly Museum on St Mary's.

Most of the present fauna and flora must have been greatly shaped by the gross selection processes of the past four or five millennia on Scilly. As far as is known, man appeared in the Isles a little before 2000 BC. At that time, according to Thomas (1985), the Scillies comprised one large central island (maximum length 12 miles, approx. breadth, 7 miles) with two extensive smaller islands close by, to the west (Thomas 1985 fig.44). This whole area seems to have been forested with oak, alder and hazel of which the last has disappeared. Very gradually, the islands were submerged leaving, in earlier stages of the process, swamp land in much of the inter-island area of today and, later, sea. These woodlands were inhabited by such species as feral deer (red and smaller species) and wild swine. The effects of deforestation on the acarine fauna, especially the Cryptostigmata, must have been immense but are always to be remembered when attempting to account for contemporary Scillonian species. Later changes might, for a few centuries, have proved cataclysmic. Thus, agriculture apart, elder trees were introduced by the monks of Tavistock, after 1120, and these were so successful that they evolved to climax vegetation on Tresco, formerly known as Innischawe (Island of the elder trees). Perhaps it would have looked not unlike Dungeness today. That, at least, could not have been conducive to the support of a rich acarine fauna.

A bibliography of the entomology (including spiders) of the Isles of Scilly is given by Smith and Smith (1983), but, apart mainly from investigations by Bristowe (1929,1935) on the spider fauna, the Arachnida has not figured prominently. Recent contributions on other invertebrate groups from Scilly are on the Pycnogonida (King 1972), the Tardigrada (King, Forby and Morgan 1981) and the Myriapoda (Jones and Pratley 1987), whilst species recorded on Scilly are included in the provisional atlases of Pseudoscorpiones (Jones 1980) and ticks (Ixodoidea) (Martyn 1988).

ACARI

To date there has been no comprehensive review of the acarine fauna of the Isles of Scilly. Pugh and King (1988) recorded 29 species (their Table 6) from Scilly in their account of the British supralittoral, but only 20 of the 77 species they list seem attributable to Scilly. Pugh (1988) recorded 38 species from Scilly in his account of 80 species of shore-dwelling Acari from a number of localities on the islands and from the south-western peninsula of the mainland (Cornwall, Devon and Dorset). More recently Luxton (1990) has listed 44 species of oribatid mites from Scilly. He collected 36 species at 14 random locations on St Mary's on the 16 July 1986 and of these 33 were new to Scilly and two were new to the British Isles. There have also been a number of papers dealing with new species found on Scilly (e.g. Turk 1948), or more wide-ranging reviews that have included species records from Scilly (e.g. Evans 1957, Evans and Hyatt 1960, Hyatt 1980, 1987, 1990 *a,c*).

The author's first visit to the Isles of Scilly in March 1957 was as a member of the team which founded the St Agnes Bird Observatory. This operated from March 1957 until the end of 1967 and detailed reports were published. Since then regular annual reports have been published by the Cornwall Bird Watching and Preservation Society. In 1957, 1958, 1959 and 1962 litter and humus were collected from a variety of habitats on St Agnes and from these samples were extracted the microarthropods by Berlese funnel desiccation technique. During and between those years, and in almost every year since, the author has collected on St Agnes any beetles seen to be harbouring mites, and the results of this particular aspect have recently been published (Hyatt 1990a). A few other mites have been collected at random, whilst a number of ticks were removed from birds during ringing activities at the Bird Observatory.

The 'island' of Gugh, which at low tide is joined to St Agnes by a sand bar, or tombolo, is considered as part of St Agnes.

It was the intention to examine in detail all the material collected and this would undoubtedly have resulted in the description of new taxa and more additions to the British list. However, the author's decision to take early retirement in early 1989 made it impossible to undertake a full examination of the collection. Nevertheless, a considerable proportion, amounting to 104 species, has been fully identified. Additionally, some 42 taxa are named to genus or family only, but that does not mean that they are new, rather that they are not conspecific with related, named species, or that they could not be identified with certainty due to their condition, or without undertaking thorough taxonomic revisions. The BM(NH) collections contain further scattered material from Scilly, and where this has come to light during the preparation of this paper it is included. All of the material collected by the author is deposited in the British Museum (Natural History).

Evans *et al.* (1961), in their table of 100 species of British littoral and estuarine Acari, indicated 80 species from the intertidal zones and from tidal debris, and of these 22 (about 27 per cent) were considered to be restricted to those habitats. Several species in their list have yet to be recorded from Scilly. Pugh and King (1988) noted that 'The supralittoral fauna of the Isles of Scilly is unusual, in that there are significantly more non-littoral species and fewer true maritime species throughout the Isles, compared with other regions . . . the location of Scilly may account for this phenomenon, where the "missing" maritime mites may not have colonized the islands'. It is of interest to note that on the smaller islands, like St Agnes, some littoral species can be found almost anywhere, due no doubt to the frequent very strong winds that spread salt spray and debris and the fact that much tidal debris, especially sandy seaweed, was, until recent years, spread over the bulb-fields as manure.

Clearly more species, both littoral and non-littoral, will be added to the Scilly list in the future, but it is surprising that so far a number of well-known littoral forms that one would have expected have not turned up. For instance, among the Mesostigmata these include *Hydrogamasus salinus* (Laboulbène) (Rhodacaridae), *Halolaelaps marinus* (Brady) (Halolaelapidae), *Pachylaelaps littoralis* Halbert (Pachylaelapidae), *Cyrthydrolaelaps hirtus* Berlese (Veigaiidae), *Vulgarogamasus trouessarti* (Berlese) and *V. immanis* (Berlese) (Parasitidae). Among the Prostigmata one species in particular, *Lucasiella plumipes* (L.Koch) (Erythraeidae), one of the plume-footed mites, might possibly be found on the islands. It has been recorded from Jersey (Browning 1956) and there is a slide in the BM(NH) in the C.F.George collection, *c.*1920, without locality data. It is known from the Biscay coast of France and widely from the Mediterranean regions of Europe and north Africa and from Sinai and Arabia. In view of the presence of a Lusitanian element in the fauna of the south-westerly mild regions of the British Isles (Corbet 1962), this species, which runs rapidly, holding its posterior pair of legs up like sails, could well occur on Scilly. However, it has been searched for extensively, mainly on the sandy beaches of St Agnes, and also on Tresco.

An interesting account of the habits of a similar species of plume-footed mite is given by Lawrence (1937), whilst delightful illustrations of a north African species are given by Pickard-Cambridge (1897). A second species that has been sought is *Vulgarogamasus immanis* (referred to above), which exceeds two millimetres in body length and is restricted to the seashore where it is found amongst debris above the tide line and under stones and shingle. In the British Isles it is recorded from Dumfries & Galloway, the Firths of Clyde and Forth, the Menai Straits, Dorset, Galway, Mayo, Dublin and Cork (Hyatt 1980, 1990c). It might also have been expected in Scilly, but it does seem to be a northern European species, being recorded also from Iceland and Norway (Hyatt 1980).

Conspicuous acarine omissions from Scilly, due to lack of collecting, include many parasites, commensals and nest inhabitants of small mammals, including bats, and birds, as well as the plant-gall mites (Prostigmata: Eriophyidae).

Sampling Locations on St Agnes, 1957-1962, K.H.Hyatt
1. Wet tidal debris above HWM, Periglis, 27.iii.1957. [KHH 164]*.

Periglis, a graded sandy beach on the north-western side of St Agnes, is a haven for waders and many passerine birds which feed on the tossed-up tidal debris which, when rotting, teems with invertebrates such as insects, mites and sandhoppers.

2. Litter under dense evergreen hedges of *Pittosporum crassifolium*, Lower Town, 28.iii.1957. [KHH 167].
3. As No. 1, 3.iv.1957. [KHH 163].
4. As No. 2, 5.iv.1957. [KHH 173].
5. Thrift, grass and mosses on rocks above HWM, Bergecooth, 7.iv.1957. [KHH 165].
6. Soil and leaves under giant tree *Echium*, Lower Town, 7.ix.1957. [KHH 171].
7. Rotting stalks and straw, Lower Town, 9.ix.1957. [KHH 168].
8. Rotting grass mowings, Lower Town, 11.ix.1957. [KHH 172].
9. Lichenous earth on rocks, Gugh, 14.ix.1957. [KHH 166].
10. As No. 2, 17.ix.1957. [KHH 169].
11. Roots of rushes, mainly *Scirpus maritimus*, Big Pool, 19.ix.1957. [KHH 170].

Lower Town Farm, St Agnes, with its small fields surrounded by tall hedges of *Pittosporum*, *Euonymus* and *Tamarix*. In the meadow is, left,the brackish Big Pool surrounded by sea clubrush *Scirpus maritimus*, whilst to the right is the less-permanent Little Pool.

12. Damp moss on rocks by Lighthouse, 26.x.1958. [KHH 174].
13. Mixed deciduous litter in Parsonage garden, 1.xi.1958. [KHH 176].
14. Rotting bracken, Higher Town, 4.xi.1958. [KHH 175].
15. Heather roots and soil, Wingletang Down, 30.x.-2.xi.1959 [KHH 179].
16. As No. 2, 5.xi.1959. [KHH 177].
17. Woody litter in Parsonage garden, 10.x.1962. [KHH 181].
18. As No. 17, x.1962. [KHH 180].
19. As No. 11, 24.x.1962. [KHH 178].

* The numbers in square brackets refer to the BM(NH) Arachnida Section data books which record details of acarine samples collected in the British Isles by many people and deposited in the Section.

Species List

+   indicates new records for the Isles of Scilly
[+]   indicates new records at family or genus level only
*   indicates species new to the British Isles.

CLASS ARACHNIDA
SUBCLASS ACARI
Order MESOSTIGMATA
Suborder GAMASINA

Family Macrochelidae

Dissoloncha superbus (Hull, 1918)
A common maritime species widely distributed in England, Wales and Scotland, but so far not recorded from Ireland although other records suggest it is holarctic in distribution (Hyatt and Emberson 1988).

Recorded from Scilly by Pugh and King (1988) on St Mary's and by Pugh (1988) on Bryher, Great Arthur, Samson and St Mary's in tidal debris and under stones in the extreme upper littoral and supralittoral zones.

Geholaspis (Geholaspis) longispinosus (Kramer, 1876)
This is one of the commonest European macrochelids, being found throughout the British Isles, whilst it is also reported from New Zealand where it is presumably adventive (Hyatt and Emberson 1988).

The same authors recorded it from Scilly based on specimens collected by the present author on St Agnes - Sample 10.

Geholaspis (Longicheles) mandibularis (Berlese, 1904)
Found throughout the British Isles and widespread in Europe in a variety of litter and soil habitats as well as in the nests of ants and small mammals (Hyatt and

Emberson 1988).

The same authors recorded it from Scilly based on specimens collected by the present author on St Agnes - Samples 2, 4, 9, 10, 12, 13.

Glyptholaspis americana (Berlese, 1888)
Apparently almost cosmopolitan in distribution: recorded from England and Ireland by Hyatt and Emberson (1988) and Hyatt (1990*a*), whose records from Scilly are on the basis of a single female on *Geotrupes spiniger*, St Agnes, 6.x.1958, coll. KHH. Elsewhere it is found generally in compost and associated with synanthropic flies.

Holostaspella ornata (Berlese, 1904)
A widespread European species first recorded from the British Isles, including the Isles of Scilly, by Hyatt and Emberson (1988). The Scilly material comprises females collected by myself on St Agnes - Samples 2, 10.

Marocheles carinatus (C.L. Koch, 1839)
A widespread European species found throughout the British Isles in a variety of damp litter habitats including flood debris, dead grass, seaweed, moss, etc. (Hyatt and Emberson 1988).

The same authors recorded it from Scilly based on males and females collected by the author on St Agnes - Samples 2, 4, 10.

Macrocheles glaber (Müller, 1860)
This widespread species is found throughout the British Isles, including Scilly, and in most temperate regions of the northern hemisphere and also in New Zealand (Hyatt and Emberson 1988). It is most often associated with coprophagus beetles.

Hyatt (1990*a*) examined 112 collections from beetles and of these, 22 were from St Agnes: 17 *Geotrupes spiniger*, three *Geotrupes stercorarius* and two *Typhaeus typhoeus*. Dispersal in this species is accomplished by the females only, which in *Macrocheles* are parthenogenic. Additional specimens (males, females and deutonymphs), also recorded by Hyatt and Emberson, were collected by the author on St Agnes - Samples 4, 7, 8, 9, 10.

+*Macrocheles submotus* Falconer, 1923
Known only from the British Isles, where it was recorded as common throughout in a wide variety of mainly damp habitats. Hyatt and Emberson (1988) inadvertantly omitted to include the author's records of protonymphs, deutonymphs, males and females from St Agnes - Sample 13.

Family Eviphididae

Alliphis halleri (G. & R. Canestrini, 1881)
This is the most abundant member of the genus *Alliphis* and is recorded widely

from Britain, central Europe, Israel and Japan at least (Hyatt 1990*a*). It is commonly carried by beetles and Hyatt (1990*a*) recorded it from seven species, although predominately from *Geotrupes spiniger* and *Geotrupes stercorarius*.

It was first recorded from Scilly by Hyatt (1959) who collected 15 deutonymphs and one female from *Geotrupes stercorarius* on St Agnes. To date the author has examined 22 collections from St Agnes of males, females and deutonymphs mainly on the above-mentioned species, but also on *Typhaeus typhoeus*, and additionally from Samples 4, 5.

+*Eviphis ostrinus* (C.L.Koch, 1836)

A widespread European species in mosses and leaf-litter over a wide range of soil types. The BM collections contain specimens from Kent, Hertfordshire, Berkshire, Cumbria (Cumberland), the Inner Hebrides (Isle of Eigg) and Scilly (as detailed below).

St Agnes - Sample 13.

Scamiphis equestris (Berlese, 1911)

This species was first recorded from the British Isles by Evans (1957). Hyatt (1959) recorded it from the Isles of Scilly based on adult specimens from *Geotrupes stercorarius* on St Agnes and has subsequently collected further adults from 10 specimens of *Goetrupes spiniger*, also on St Agnes (Hyatt 1990*a*).

Scarabaspis inexpectatus (Oudemans,1903)

This species was first recorded from the British Isles by Evans (1957) based on specimens from *Geotrupes stercorarius* collected by the author on St Agnes. Hyatt (1990*a*) recorded it from widely scattered localities in England and Wales, mainly from *Geotrupes*.

To date the author has examined 12 specimens of *Geotrupes spiniger*, two *Geotrupes stercorarius* and one *Typhaeus typhoeus* from St Agnes, most carrying only a few specimens, but one of the *stercorarius* was harbouring 46 deutonymphs, 20 males and 67 females.

Thinoseius fucicola (Halbert, 1920)

Members of the genus Thinoseius inhabit decaying seaweed and other decaying tidal debris above high-water mark. The present species was described from Malahide, Co. Dublin and Swanage, Dorset.

It was first recorded from Scilly by Pugh and King (1988) from St Mary's and by Pugh (1988) who examined specimens from Bryher, Great Arthur and St Mary's.

My own collections from St Agnes are from Samples 1, 2, 3.

Family Pachylaelapidae

+***Pachylaelaps denticulatus* Hirschmann & Krauss,1965
This European species has not previously been recorded from the British Isles.
Many males and females on St Agnes - Samples 4, 5, 6, 12, 13, 14.

+*Pachylaelaps longisetis* Halbert, 1915
This is the most common species of *Pachylaelaps* in humus and rotting wood
in the British Isles (Evans and Hyatt 1956). It is widespread in Europe (Karg
1971) and the USSR (Bregetova *et al.* 1977).
Males and females from St Agnes - Samples 12, 14, 15.

+*Pachylaelaps sellnicki* Hirschmann & Krauss,1965
This European species was recorded from Berkshire by Evans and Hyatt (1956)
as *P. lindrothi* Sellnick, 1940. However this was, according to Hirschmann and
Krauss (1965), a misidentification.
Several females from St Agnes - Samples 4, 5, 6.

+*Pachylaelaps undulatus* Evans & Hyatt, 1956
Described originally from rotting wood in Hertfordshire and pondside debris
in Middlesex, this species has since been collected in Kent, Surrey, Essex and
Northamptonshire.
Females from St Agnes - Samples 4, 5, 6.

+*Pachylaelaps* sp.
Several unidentified specimens from St Agnes - Sample 2.

+*Pachyseius angustus* Hyatt, 1956
Described from leaf-litter and lakeside debris in northern England (Hyatt
1956*b*).
A single female collected on St Agnes - Sample 17.

+*Pachyseius humeralis* Berlese, 1910
A European species first recorded from the British Isles by Hyatt (1956*b*) who
collected specimens in beech litter at Box Hill, Surrey.
Several females collected on St Agnes - Sample 2.

Family Phytoseiidae

[+]*Amblyseius* sp.
An unidentified specimen from St Agnes - Sample 9.

Anthoseius sp.
Recorded from Scilly by Pugh and King (1988) from Tresco and St Mary's and
by Pugh (1988) who examined specimens from supralittoral lichens, particularly
Xanthorina parietina (L.), on Bryher, Tresco and St Mary's.

Family Ameroseiidae

+Epicriopsis horridus (Kramer, 1876)
A widespread inhabitant of woodland litter and usually damp humus in Europe and the USSR. It is widely distributed, but rather infrequent, in the British Isles.
Collected on St Agnes from Sample 6.

Kleemannia plumigera (Oudemans, 1930)
A widespread, mycophagous European species found largely in damp, mouldy situations such as cracks in the walls of buildings. Also recorded from grain debris and broiler-house litter (Hughes, 1976).
Collected on St Agnes from Samples 7, 8, 9; also from under the elytra of *Geotrupes stercorarius*, 10.ix.1957 (Hyatt 1990a).

+Kleemannia plumosus (Oudemans, 1902)
This widespread European species, which is recorded also from Australia and Canada, is found usually in situations such as manure, rotting vegetables, bumblebee, ant and small mammal nests, under haystacks, in stored grain debris and in broiler-house litter.
Collected on St Agnes from Samples 7, 8, 11, 12.

+Kleemannia sp.
A single unidentified female from St Agnes - Sample 8.

Family Halolaelapidae

+Halolaelaps celticus Halbert, 1915
All species of *Halolaelaps* are intertidal or estuarine and often occur abundantly in tidal debris. Their deutonymphs use sandhoppers (Amphipoda) for dispersal. This species was described from specimens collected under stones below high tide line at Westport, Co. Mayo and it was recorded subsequently (Halbert 1920) at Howth, Co. Dublin amongst decaying seaweeds, whilst Hull (1918) recorded it from Bamburgh, Northumberland. Hyatt (1956a) recorded it as widely distributed in tidal debris in the British Isles.
Collected abundantly (males, females and deutonymphs) on St Agnes - Samples 1, 3,18.

Halolaelaps incisus Hyatt, 1956
Described (Hyatt 1956a) from specimens collected in wrack at Sea Houses, Northumberland and recorded subsequently from northern and central Europe (Karg 1971).
Pugh (1988) recorded it from Dorset and on Scilly from tidal debris on St Mary's.

Family Ascidae

Arctoseoides ibericus (Willmann, 1949)
A littoral species described originally from Spain, Pugh (1988) recorded it from Scilly based on specimens collected on Annet in association with barnacles and lichens.

Cheiroseius cassiteridum (Evans & Hyatt, 1960)
Described from specimens collected on St Agnes - Sample 11 - and from a single female from *Sphagnum*, Blelham Tarn, Lancashire, this species does not appear to have been recorded since.

Lasioseius confusus Evans, 1958
Described from material collected on St Agnes - Sample 11 - and from *Sphagnum*, Cors Fochno, Dyfed, this species has now been recorded from mainland Europe and the USSR (Bregetova *et al.* 1977).

Neojordensia levis (Voigts & Oudemans, 1904)
A widespread European species recorded from damp habitats in Britain and Ireland.
        Evans (1958) examined specimens collected by the present author from St Agnes - Sample 11.

Platyseius subglaber (Oudemans, 1903)
A western European species, probably widely distributed in the British Isles, and recorded from Scilly (Evans and Hyatt 1960) based on specimens collected by the present author on St Agnes - Sample 11.

[+]*Proctolaelaps* sp.
Several specimens from St Agnes - Sample 7.

+*Zerconopsis remiger* (Kramer, 1876)
First recorded in the British Isles from Ireland by Halbert (1915), then in Northumberland by Hull (1918) and later in Cheshire, Westmorland, Middlesex and Gloucestershire (Evans and Hyatt 1960).
        Collected now on St Agnes - Samples 7, 10.

+*Zercoseius spathuliger* (Leonardi, 1899)
A widely distributed European species found in a variety of habitats including pinewoods, deciduous litter, compost and humus. Recorded from Britain (Evans 1958) and Jersey (Browning 1956).
        Collected on St Agnes from Sample 9.

Family Laelapidae

+*Androlaelaps casalis casalis* (Berlese, 1887)
A well-known, cosmopolitan predator found frequently in birds' nests, poultry

litter and on rodents (Evans and Till 1966).
   Collected now on St Agnes - Sample 7.

+*Cosmolaelaps claviger* (Berlese, 1883)
A widespread, probably predacious, species, living in soil, litter and rotting wood and recorded from Britain and Europe (Evans and Till 1966).
   Collected on St Agnes from Samples 5, 9, 12.

+**Gymnolaelaps austriaca* (Sellnick, 1935)
Described originally in association with *Formica rufa* in Austria and subsequently recorded from central Europe in moss, lichen and rotting wood (Karg 1971).
   Several females collected on St Agnes - Sample 5.
   This is the first record for the British Isles.

+*Hypoaspis aculeifer* (Canestrini, 1884)
A holarctic species, common in soil and litter and found occasionally in the nests of birds and small mammals (Evans and Till 1966) and also in stored foodstuffs.
   Recorded now from St Agnes - Samples 2, 4, 10, 12.

Hypoaspis krameri (G. & R. Canestrini, 1881)
A European species, previously recorded from Britain by Evans and Till (1966), Hyatt (1990*a*) detailed the British records which included one female from *Typhaeus typhoeus*, St Agnes, 2.xi.1959.

+*Hypoaspis vacua* (Michael, 1891)
A widespread European species recorded from the British Isles in a wide variety of habitats including mosses, leaf-litter and in ants' nests (Evans and Till 1966).
   Collected now on St Agnes - Sample 5.

+*Hypoaspis* sp.
Two unidentified females, St Agnes - Sample 4.

+*Pseudoparasitus centralis* Berlese, 1921
Free living in litter under deciduous trees, etc. in Britain and Europe (Evans and Till 1966).
   Collected on St Agnes from Samples 8, 9, 10, 11, 12.

+Family Rhodacaridae

+*Rhodacarus roseus* Oudemans, 1902
A very common Palaearctic species, widely distributed in the British Isles.
   Recorded now from St Agnes - Samples 4, 9, 10.

[+]Family Digmasellidae

[+]*Dendrolaelaps* sp.
Two unidentified females from St Agnes - Sample 12.

Family Veigaiidae

+*Veigaia exigua* (Berlese, 1916)
This European species has only recently been reported from the British Isles.
Till (1988) recorded a single female from Co. Wexford and Hyatt (1990*b*)
recorded 19 specimens (males and females) from Headley Heath, Surrey.
        Several specimens collected on St Agnes - Sample 9.

+*Veigaia nemorensis* (C.L.Koch, 1839)
A widespread Palaearctic species common in the British Isles in coniferous and
deciduous litter, in moss and in grassland.
        Collected on St Agnes from Samples 5, 11.

+*Veigaia planicola* (Berlese, 1892)
A common and widespread Palaearctic species found in leaf-litter and humus
and recorded from the British Isles.
        Collected on St Agnes from the following Samples - 4, 5, 6, 9, 12, 13.

Family Parasitidae

Subfamily Parasitinae

***Cornigamasus lunaris* (Berlese, 1882)**
This European species is widely distributed in the British Isles and is found
mainly in compost, vegetable refuse, manure, haystacks and the like. Halbert
(1915,1920) recorded it from decaying seaweeds on the shore, but observed that
this was probably not its normal habitat.
        Hyatt (1980) recorded it from Scilly based on deutonymphs, males and
females from St Agnes - Samples 7, 8.

***Gamasodes fimbriatus* Karg, 1971**
A seashore species, described from the Baltic, and first recorded from the
British Isles by Hyatt (1980) who examined material from England, Scotland,
Wales and Ireland.
        His records from the Isles of Scilly were based on deutonymphs, males
and females from St Agnes - Samples 1, 3, 18. Pugh and King (1988) and Pugh
(1988) recorded it from supralittoral lichens on Tresco.

***Parasitellus fucorum* (De Geer, 1778)**
This common European species is almost certainly distributed throughout the

British Isles. With few exceptions it is found on bumblebees *Bombus* spp. However, the only record the author knows of from Scilly is three deutonymphs on *Bombus muscorum*, St Mary's, 20.vii.1925, O.W.Richards coll. (Hyatt 1980).

Parasitus coleoptratorum (Linnaeus, 1758)

This species is widespread in the British Isles and was recorded from Scilly by Hyatt (1980) who noted its occurrence throughout Europe, in the USSR, the Middle East and Chile. The deutonymphs are well-known paraphages of Coleoptera (Hyatt 1959, 1980, 1990*a*) whereas the adults, which are found much less frequently, are confined mainly to compost, manure and rich humus including seaweed (Hyatt 1980).

From St Agnes the author has examined deutonymphs from 21 beetles - 15 *Geotrupes spiniger*, four *G. stercorarius* and two *Typhaeus typhoeus* - and males, females and deutonymphs from Sample 8.

Parasitus consanguineus Oudemans & Voigts, 1904

This species is widespread in Europe and occurs throughout the British Isles. Hyatt (1980) recorded it from Scilly based on a deutonymph, males and females in leaf-litter and rotting straw, Samples 4, 7, 10. Normally it is found in 'richer' habitats such as manure, compost and decaying vegetables.

Parasitus copridis Costa, 1963

This species, which was known previously from Israel and Western Siberia, was first recorded in the British Isles by Hyatt (1980) who examined 111 deutonymphs from 12 beetles, eight *Geotrupes spiniger* and four *G. stercorosus*. Four of the *spiniger* (coll. 1958-1963) and one of the *stercorosus* (coll. 1979) were collected by myself on St Agnes.

Parasitus fimetorum (Berlese, 1904)

This is one of the most widespread European species of *Parasitus* and is distributed throughout the British Isles. Hyatt (1980) recorded it from Scilly based on material collected on St Agnes -Samples 2, 4, 7, 8, 10.

Parasitus insignis (Holzmann, 1969)

Described from house-plant soil at Erlangen, Germany and recorded subsequently from clay loam with rye-grass in Berkshire (Hyatt 1980), the author has subsequently examined a single male from orchard compost at Cooksbridge, Sussex (Hyatt 1990*b*).

Pugh (1988) has collected it in tidal debris on St Mary's.

Parasitus kempersi Oudemans, 1902

This often abundant and exclusively seashore European species is probably found throughout the British Isles. Hyatt (1980) recorded it from Scilly based on collections from St Agnes where it was found in large numbers in tidal debris above HWM and also in leaf-litter, etc. below hedges some distance from the shore, Samples 1, 2, 3, 5, 7.

Pugh and King (1988) recorded it from St Mary's and Pugh (1988) examined specimens from Bryher, Tresco, St Martin's, Great Arthur and St Mary's.

Parasitus loricatus (Wankel, 1861)
A widespread European species, distributed throughout the British Isles. Hyatt (1980) recorded it from Scilly based on deutonymphs, males and females collected on St Agnes - Samples 4, 7.

Parasitus mustelarum Oudemans, 1902
A widespread European species first recorded from the British Isles by Hyatt (1959) as *'Parasitus* nr. *intermedius'*. Hyatt (1980) examined six samples from St Agnes, all deutonymphs, on *Geotrupes spiniger*, and since then has examined a further deutonymph from *G. stercorarius*, also on St Agnes, 7.iv.1982 (Hyatt 1990*a*).

+*Poecilochirus carabi* G. & R. Canestrini, 1882
This widespread Palaearctic species is found mainly as deutonymphs phoretic on *Nicrophorus* beetles and although widely distributed in the British Isles, Hyatt (1980) did not record it from Scilly.

However, the author has recently examined 10 deutonymphs from *Nicrophorus interruptus* on Tresco, viii.1950 and one deutonymph from the burrow of a puffin *Fratercula arctica* on Annet, 6.vi.1945, all collected by Dr F.A.Turk.

Porrhostaspis lunulata (Müller, 1859)
This widespread European species is distributed throughout the British Isles and is found in a wide range of habitats, e.g. leafmould, grassland, compost, mushroom beds and, rarely, seaweed and in small mammal nests.

Hyatt (1980) recorded it from Scilly on the basis of a deutonymph and females collected on St Agnes - Samples 2, 17.

Vulgarogamasus halophilus (Willmann, 1957)
Described from the Baltic coast, Pugh (1988) collected a single male from supralittoral lichens on Bryher, 12.vii.1986. Hyatt (1990*c*) has redescribed and figured Willmann's syntype specimens.

Subfamily Pergamasinae

Holoparasitus lawrencei Hyatt, 1987
This species was described from mainly damp habitats in England, Scotland, Wales and Ireland. A single female was collected on St Agnes - Sample 16.

Holoparasitus maritimus Hyatt, 1987
Described from coastal habitats in England, Scotland and Jersey. Two males were collected on St Agnes - Sample 5.

Holoparasitus stramenti Karg, 1971
Described originally from the Baltic coast and central Europe, Hyatt (1987) recorded it widely from the British Isles, including Jersey and the Isles of Scilly. Halbert (1915) and Browning (1956) had recorded it as *H. pollicipatus* (Berlese), a distinct species.
    The material from Scilly was collected on St Agnes - Samples 5, 7.

Paragamasus cambriensis (Bhattacharyya, 1963)
Described from several collections from the Midlands, southern England and Wales, including six males and 13 females collected by the author on St Agnes - Sample 2.

Paragamasus cassiteridum (Bhattacharyya, 1963)
Described from specimens from Moel Siabod in Gwynedd and from St Agnes, Isles of Scilly, author's Sample 2.

Paragamasus diversus (Halbert, 1915)
Bhattacharyya (1963) identified this species from a wide range of localities in southern England and Wales and from Co. Kerry, Ireland. These included specimens collected by the author on St Agnes - Samples 2, 4.

+*Paragamasus runciger* (Berlese, 1904)
A widespread European species. Previous British records show that it is found over much of England and from South Wales (Bhattacharyya 1963), whilst Hull (1918) recorded it from the Tyne Province, and Halbert (1915) from Ireland.
    Recorded now from St Agnes - Sample 2.

Paragamsus schweizeri (Bhattacharyya, 1963)
Described from a number of localities in England and Wales and from one locality in mid Scotland, the type series contained 29 males and 24 females collected by the author on St Agnes - Samples 2, 4.

Pergamasus longicornis (Berlese, 1906)
Specimens of this common British and European species were recorded by Bhattacharyya (1963) from material collected by the author on St Agnes - Samples 2, 4.

Pergamasus quisquiliarum (G. & R. Canestrini, 1882)
This widespread British and European species was recorded from Scilly by Bhattacharyya (1963) based on the author's specimens from St Agnes - Sample 2.

Pergamasus septentrionalis (Oudemans, 1902)
Another very widespread British and European species recorded from Scilly by Bhattacharyya (1963) based on the author's specimens from St Agnes - Sample 2.

Suborder UROPODINA

Superfamily Polyaspidoidea

Family Polyaspididae

+*Polyaspis patavinus* Berlese, 1881
A widespread European species. The genus *Polyaspis* was first recorded in the British Isles by Evans and Till (1979) based on specimens in the BM(NH) collections as noted by Hyatt (1990a) who recorded *c*.30 deutonymphs from a male stag beetle *Lucanus cervus*, Hammersmith, London and from leaf-litter at Downe, Kent.
        Now recorded from St Agnes - Sample 2.

Superfamily Uropodoidea

In a recent paper on mites associated with beetles (Hyatt 1990a) the author has stated that he was not attempting to give determinations to the uropodoids as the British fauna is urgently in need of revision and all the specimens then being considered were phoretic deutonymphs. However, a number of species can be identified with reasonable accuracy when adults are available and the determinations which follow are made with this in mind. Following Evans and Till (1979) suprageneric divisions are not included.

+*Dinychura cordieri* (Berlese, 1916)
A widespread European species already known from the British Isles. Now recorded from the Isles of Scilly: St Agnes - Sample 10.

*+*Discourella franzi* Hirschmann & Zirngiebl-Nicol, 1969
Described from Spain, but no habitat data given, this species does not appear to have been recorded since. Now recorded from the British Isles based on numerous deutonymphs, males and females from St Agnes - Samples 2, 4, 5, 6, 10, 12.

[+]*Discourella sp.*
A second species of this genus from St Agnes - Samples 3, 4, 5, 6.

+*Leiodinychus punctata* (Hirschmann & Zirngiebl-Nicol, 1961)
A European species already known from the British Isles. Now recorded from the Isles of Scilly : St Agnes - Sample 10.

+*Olodiscus minima* (Kramer, 1882)
A common European species found mainly in humus and leaf-litter and probably distributed throughout the British Isles where suitable habitats occur.

Recorded now from the Isles of Scilly based on males, females and a few deutonymphs from St Agnes - Samples 2, 3, 4, 6, 8, 9, 10, 12, 13.

+*Oodinychus ovalis* (C.L.Koch, 1839)
A European species already known from the British Isles. Now recorded from the Isles of Scilly: St Agnes - Sample 7.

[+]*Phaulocylliba* sp.
Unidentified specimens from St Agnes - Sample 5.

+*Phaulodinychus minor* (Halbert, 1915)
Described originally and recorded subsequently (Halbert 1920) from the seashore in Cos Mayo and Dublin, the present collections from St Agnes comprise many deutonymphs and adults from Samples 1, 3, 5, 18.

Phaulodinychus orchestiidarum (Barrois, 1887)
A well-known European littoral species recorded from Ireland by Halbert (1920) and from Scilly by Pugh and King (1988) and by Pugh (1988) from tidal debris on St Mary's.

+*Phaulodinychus pulcherrima* (Berlese, 1904)
A common European species found mainly in soil, rotting wood and in ants' nests. Collected on St Agnes from Samples 8, 10.

Phaulodinychus repletus Berlese, 1903
Described originally from Norway (no habitat given), this maritime species was first recorded in the British Isles from Ireland as *Haluropoda interrupta* by Halbert (1915). Hull (1918) recorded it from the Tyne Province and Halbert (1920) added more Irish records.

Pugh (1988) recorded it from tidal debris and under stones in the extreme upper littoral on St Mary's. The author has collected many protonymphs, deutonymphs and adults from tidal debris, grass and moss and under hedges on St Agnes - Samples 1, 2, 3, 5.

[+]*Phaulodinychus* spp.
At least five more species of this genus have been collected on St Agnes, viz. Sp. A - Samples 1, 3, 5; Sp. B - Samples 3, 5; Sp. C - Samples 3, 5; Sp. D - Samples 3, 5; Sp. E - Samples 2, 4, 10.

*+*Uroobovella appendiculata* (Berlese, 1910)
Described originally from Florence, Italy, this species has not previously been recorded in the British Isles. Females only collected by the author on St Agnes

- Samples 5, 12.

+*Uropoda orbicularis* (Müller, 1776)
A common European species well recorded from the British Isles. Collected on St Agnes (deutonymphs and adults) from Samples 2, 4, 6, 7, 8, 10, 11, and also deutonymphs from *Geotrupes stercorarius*, on grass, Troy Town, St Agnes, 1.iv.1957.

*+*Uropoda vulgaris* Hirschmann & Zirngiebl-Nicol, 1969
Described from *Sphagnum* and under shrubs in Spain, now recorded for the first time from the British Isles on St Agnes - Sample 5.

*+*Uropoda willmanni* Hirschmann & Zirngiebl-Nicol, 1969
Described from leaf-litter in Germany, now recorded for the first time in the British Isles from St Agnes - Samples 3, 4, 6, 8, 9, 10.

Order METASTIGMATA (IXODOIDEA) - Ticks

Family Ixodidae

Ixodes acuminatus Neumann, 1901
This is a widespread European species whose occurrence in the British Isles seems limited to south-west England. *Ixodes dorriensmithi* Turk, 1948, which was described from Scilly (St Mary's and Tresco), is considered to be a synonym of *I. acuminatus* (Martyn 1988). On Scilly it is found mainly on the lesser white-toothed shrew *Crocidura suaveolens cassiteridum*. The author has seen specimens from this host from Tresco and St Agnes, also from *Apodemus sylvaticus* on St Mary's, and from *Rattus norvegicus* and *Mus domesticus* on St Agnes.

Ixodes apronophorus Schulze, 1924
Found throughout northern Europe, but uncommon in Britain (Martyn 1988). Recorded from Scilly as *Ixodes arvicolae* Warburton, 1926 from *Crocidura suaveolens cassiteridum* and *Apodemus sylvaticus* on Tresco and St Mary's and from *Mus domesticus* on St Agnes by Rood and Burtt (1965). However, Martyn (1988) whilst accepting that *I. arvicolae* is a synonym of *I. apronophorus*, omits to include the Scilly and Cornwall records of Rood and Burtt.

Ixodes frontalis Panzer, 1805
Widely distributed throughout Europe, this is exclusively a parasite of birds, mainly passerines. Males have not been found in the British Isles, but elsewhere have been reported from the undergrowth beneath trees used by nesting birds (Martyn 1988). Of the 150 samples examined by Martyn, including those from Scilly detailed below, the blackbird accounted for 38 with greenfinch next with 14.

The BM(NH) collections contain two nymphs from leaf-litter on St Agnes - Samples 2, 4, and the following records from birds: from Tresco ex linnet, ix.1965; from St Agnes ex blackbird, song thrush and blue tit, x.1957, and house sparrow, x.1959.

Ixodes trianguliceps Birula, 1895
This widely distributed European species is common in Britain, but relatively scarce in Ireland where it is replaced principally by *Ixodes ricinus*, the 'sheep tick' (Martyn 1988). It is exclusively a parasite of small, burrowing mammals of which the bank vole and wood mouse appear to be the commonest hosts (Martyn 1988).

The BM(NH) collections contain three samples from Scilly: from *Crocidura suaveolens cassiteridum* on Tresco, 15.iii.1961 and St Agnes, 11.vii. 1964, and from *Apodemus sylvaticus* on St Mary's, 15.iii.1961.

Ixodes unicavatus Neumann, 1908
This species is restricted to north-west Europe where it usually parasitizes marine and coastal birds. Martyn (1988) recorded it from Scilly based on two females from a cormorant, Mincarlo, 16.v.1946, coll. F.A.Turk.

Ixodes ventalloi Gil Collado, 1936
This is principally an Iberian species which has spread to France, Germany and north Africa. It is rare in Britain and has so far been found only in the Channel Islands, Lundy and Scilly where it was probably introduced with rabbits. The only other recorded British hosts of this species are cat and long-eared owl, both of which would be predators of rabbits (Martyn 1988).

Samples from Scilly are from rabbits: Tresco, ii & v.1964 and St Agnes, xi.1964.

Order CRYPTISTOGMATA (ORIBATEI)

+Family Euphthiracaridae

+*Rhysotritia ardua* (C.L.Koch, 1841)
Widespread in England and Wales from a wide range of habitats, e.g. coniferous and deciduous woodland, *Calluna* heathland and *Sphagnum* bogs (Luxton pers. comm.).
St Agnes - Sample 2.

+*Rhysotritia duplicata* (Grandjean, 1953)
Widely recorded in England, but not in the extreme south and south-west, from Scotland (no data) and from Co. Clare, Ireland, in grassland, moorland, in mosses and in deciduous litter (Luxton pers. comm.).
St Agnes - Samples 2, 4.

Family Phthiracaridae

Phthiracarus affinis (Hull, 1914)
Widespread and abundant in the British Isles (Luxton 1990). Recorded from Scilly by Parry (1979) and Luxton (1990) based on specimens collected by myself on St Agnes - Samples 4, 10.

+*Phthiracarus anonymus* (Grandjean, 1934)
Widely recorded in England, from Gwent in Wales, Strathclyde in Scotland and from the north and south-east of Ireland, mainly in damp habitats, but also in coniferous and deciduous litter (Luxton pers. comm.).
St Agnes - Sample 2.

Phthiracarus nitens (Nicolet, 1855)
Recorded in the British Isles from southern England and the Channel Islands (Luxton 1990). Recorded from Scilly by Parry (1979) and Luxton (1990) based on specimens collected by the author on St Agnes - Sample 4.

[+]Family Hypochthoniidae

[+]*Hypochthonius* spp.
This genus is represented in the British Isles by two species, the commonest being *Hypochthonius rufulus* C.L.Koch, 1836 (Luxton pers. comm.).
Unidentified specimens representing one or more species from St Agnes - Samples 2, 13.

Family Hermanniidae

Hermannia reticulata (Thorell, 1871)
Widespread and common in the British Isles, collected on Scilly by Luxton (1990) from lichen, moss and thrift from The Garrison, St Mary's. Collected on St Agnes from Samples 9, 12.

Hermannia scabra (L.Koch, 1879)
Widespread and common in the British Isles, collected on Scilly by Luxton (1990) from mosses at Hugh Town, St Mary's. Collected on St Agnes from Samples 2, 4, 8, 10, 13.

Hermannia sp.
Unidentified specimens from St Agnes - Samples 2, 3, 4, 5, 7, 8, 9, 11.

Family Camisiidae

Camisia biverrucata (C.L.Koch, 1839)
Widespread, but not common, in England and Scotland, not recorded from

Ireland or Wales, collected on Scilly by Luxton (1990) from thrift on The Garrison, St Mary's.

Camisia horrida (Hermann, 1804)
Widespread and common in the British Isles, collected on Scilly by Luxton (1990) from moss and lichen on St Mary's.

Camisia segnis (Hermann, 1804)
An essentially non-maritime European species, widespread and common in the British Isles (Luxton 1990). Recorded from St Mary's by Pugh and King (1988) and from St Mary's and Annet by Pugh (1988) among supralittoral yellow lichens.

+*Platynothrus peltifer* (C.L.Koch, 1839)
Widespread and common in the British Isles (Luxton 1989).
    St Agnes - Sample 8.

[+]Family Malaconothridae

Unidentified specimens, probably of one species, collected by the author on St Agnes - Sample 5.

+Family Nothridae

+*Nothrus biciliatus* C.L.Koch, 1841
Previously known from a *Molinia* fen in Oxfordshire (Macfadyen 1952) and from leaf-litter in Cambridgeshire (Luxton pers. comm.).
    St Agnes - Samples 1, 4, 13.

+*Nothrus palustris* C.L.Koch, 1839
Widespread and common in the British Isles (Luxton 1989).
    St Agnes: many nymphs and adults from Sample 13.

+*Nothrus silvestris* Nicolet, 1855
Widely distributed in England, from North Wales, locally in Scotland and in the west of Ireland (Luxton pers. comm.).
    St Agnes - Samples 1, 5.

Nothrus sp.
Unidentified specimens collected on St Agnes from Sample 4.

[+]Family Hydrozetidae

[+]*Hydrozetes* sp.
Luxton (pers. comm.) records *Hydrozetes lacustris* (Michael) and *H. lemnae*

(de Coggi), inhabitants of fresh or brackish water, from the British Isles. St Agnes - Sample 11.

[+]Family Limnozetidae

[+]*Limnozetes* sp.
Luxton (pers. comm.) records two species from the British Isles: *Limnozetes rugosus* (Sellnick) from Ireland (Curry 1976) and *L. sphagni* (Michael) from England, Scotland and Ireland.
St Agnes - Samples 5, 8.

Family Ameronothridae

Ameronothrus maculatus (Michael, 1884)
Widespread and common in the British Isles (Luxton 1990). Recorded from supralittoral lichens on Tresco and St Mary's by Pugh and King (1988) and on Bryher, Tresco, St Martin's, Great Arthur, St Agnes and Annet by Pugh (1988). Luxton (1990) collected it from lichens and grass on Porthcressa Beach, St Mary's.

Hygroribates marinus (Banks, 1896)
Widespread and common in the British Isles (Luxton 1990), and recorded from Scilly by Pugh (1988) who collected specimens among lichens and barnacles in the littoral zone of Annet.

Hygroribates schneideri (Oudemans, 1905)
A European species, recorded in the British Isles from England and Wales only (Luxton 1990). Pugh and King (1988) and Pugh (1988) recorded it from supralittoral lichens on Tresco. Luxton (1990) referred to it being recorded on St Mary's by Pugh and King (1988) who in their Table 5 indicated New Grimsby to be on St Mary's when in fact it is on Tresco.

[+]Family Cymbaeremaeidae

[+]*Cymbaeremaeus* sp.
Unidentified specimens from St Agnes - Sample 5.

Family Belbidae

Metabelba papillipes (Nicolet, 1855)
Luxton (1990) considered this species to be widespread and common in the British Isles and collected specimens from bracken and thrift at The Garrison, St Mary's. The author has collected specimens on St Agnes - Sample 2.

[+]*Metabelba* sp.
Unidentified specimens also from St Agnes - Sample 2.

Family Damaeidae

Damaeus (Paradamaeus) clavipes (Hermann, 1804)
Considered by Luxton (1990) to be widespread and common in the British Isles and collected by him from bracken litter on The Garrison, St Mary's. Collected on St Agnes - Sample 5.

[+]*Damaeus* spp.
Two unidentified species, each from several samples on St Agnes. Sp. A from Samples 2, 5, 6, 7, 8, 10, 12. Sp. B from Samples 3, 4, 5, 6, 7, 9.
 Also two further species of Damaeidae, one well exceeding 1,000 μm, the other considerably smaller, from St Agnes - Sample 13.

Family Carabodidae

+*Carabodes marginatus* (Michael, 1884)
Widespread in England, Scotland and Wales, including the Isle of Man and Orkney (Luxton 1987, 1989). Not recorded from Ireland.
 Collected on St Agnes from Samples 2, 5, 6, 7, 9.

Odontocepheus elongatus (Michael, 1879)
Luxton (1990) considered this species to be widespread and common in the British Isles, although it has not been recorded from Wales, and he collected specimens from bracken litter on The Garrison, St Mary's.

Family Tectocepheidae

Tectocepheus velatus (Michael, 1880)
A widespread and very common British species collected from mosses, grasses, etc. at several sites on St Mary's (Luxton 1990).

Tectocepheus sp.
Unidentified specimens from St Agnes - Samples 5, 9, 12, could belong to the previous species.

Family Eremaeidae

Eremaeus oblongus (C.L.Koch, 1835)
A common species in the British Isles, although not recorded from Scotland, was collected from moss and soil at Hugh Town, St Mary's by Luxton (1990).
 Numerous unidentified specimens of a single species of Eremaeidae collected on St Agnes - Sample 12.

Family Ctenobelbidae

Ctenobelba obsoleta (C.L.Koch, 1841)
A reasonably common species in the British Isles, although not recorded from Wales, has been collected on Scilly from moss and soil at Hugh Town and from bracken litter on The Garrison, St Mary's (Luxton 1990)

Family Ceratoppiidae

Ceratoppia bipilis (Hermann, 1804)
Widespread and very common in the British Isles (Luxton 1990).
    Collected in bracken litter on The Garrison, St Mary's (Luxton 1990) and on St Agnes - Sample 8, 11.

Family Liacaridae

Xenillus tegeocranus (Hermann, 1804)
Widespread and common in the British Isles, although not recorded from Scotland (Luxton 1990).
    Collected in bracken litter on The Garrison, St Mary's (Luxton 1990) and on St Agnes from Samples 2, 8.
    Further specimens of Liacaridae, apparently not this species, also from St Agnes - Samples 12, 13.

Family Oppiidae

Dissorhina ornata (Oudemans, 1900)
Considered by Luxton (1990) to be widespread and common in the British Isles, though not recorded from Wales, and collected by him from moss, bracken litter and thrift at Hugh Town and on The Garrison, St Mary's.

Lauroppia neerlandica (Oudemans, 1900)
Widespread, but not common, in England and Scotland, though not recorded from Wales or Ireland; collected from dry moss on granite at Hugh Town, St Mary's (Luxton 1990).

Medioppia obsoleta (Paoli, 1908)
Widespread and common in the British Isles, although not recorded from Wales; collected from bracken litter at The Garrison, St Mary's (Luxton 1990).

Moritzoppia unicarinata (Paoli, 1908)
Previously recorded in the British Isles from England and the Isle of Man only, it has now been collected from thrift on The Garrison, St Mary's (Luxton 1990).

[+]*Oppia* spp.
Numerous unidentified specimens of one or more species collected on St Agnes
from Samples 1, 2, 3, 4, 5, 6, 7, 8, 9, 10.

Ramusella assimilis (Mihelčić, 1956)
A central European species first recorded from the British Isles by Luxton
(1990) who collected specimens from thrift on The Garrison, St Mary's.

Family Suctobelbidae

Suctobelbella subcornigera (Forsslund, 1941)
Widespread and common in the British Isles, though not recorded from Wales,
and collected from bracken litter on The Garrison, St Mary's (Luxton 1990).

Family Ceratozetidae

Ceratozetes gracilis (Michael, 1884)
A widespread and very common species in the British Isles, recorded in the Isles
of Scilly from lichen and moss under a hedge and from thrift on The Garrison,
St Mary's (Luxton 1990).

Ceratozetes sp.
Unidentified specimens which could belong to the previous species, St Agnes
- Sample 4.

Humerobates rostrolamellatus Grandjean, 1936
In the British Isles recorded from England and Wales where it is reasonably
common (Luxton 1990) and from the Isle of Man (Luxton 1987).
     Recorded form the Isles of Scilly by Luxton (1990) who collected
specimens on St Mary's from moss on stones on The Garrison and from lichens
on a lane wall.

+*Latilamellobates incisellus* (Kramer, 1897)
Widely recorded in England, Wales and Ireland (Luxton pers. comm.),
including the Isle of Man (Luxton 1987).
     Collected on St Agnes from Samples 3, 5, 9.

Trichoribates trimaculatus (C.L.Koch, 1836)
A reasonably common species, but recorded in the British Isles from England
and Scotland only (Luxton 1990).
     First recorded from Scilly by Pugh and King (1988) from tidal debris and
from supralittoral lichens on Tresco and St Mary's and by Pugh (1988) from St
Mary's, Tresco, Bryher, St Martins, Great Arthur, St Agnes and Annet. Luxton
(1990) collected three samples at Porthcressa Beach, St Mary's, on lichens and

grass.
  Collected on St Agnes from Samples 1, 2, 3, 8.

[+]*Trichoribates* sp.
Unidentified specimens from several samples on St Agnes, including tidal
debris - Samples 1, 2, 5, 8, 9, 10, 12.

Family Chamobatidae

Chamobates cuspidatus (Michael, 1884)
A widespread and common species in the British Isles, collected on Scilly by
Luxton (1990) who examined specimens from bracken litter on The Garrison,
St Mary's.

Chamobates schuetzi (Oudemans, 1902)
A widespread and common species in the British Isles, recorded from Scilly by
Luxton (1990) who collected specimens from dry moss at Hugh Town, St
Mary's.

Chamobates sp.
Unidentified specimens collected on St Agnes - Samples 2, 6,10.

+Family Euzetidae

+*Euzetes globulus* (Nicolet, 1855)
Evans *et al.* (1961) listed this species as an inhabitant of tidal debris, but noted
that it is also recorded in non-littoral habitats. Luxton (1989) considered it to
be 'Among the commonest of oribatid mites in the British Isles'.
  It is now recorded from the Isles of Scilly where specimens were
collected on St Agnes from the following Samples - 2, 4, 5, 6, 8, 10, 11, 12, 13.

Family Mycobatidae

Mycobates parmeliae (Michael, 1884)
Described originally from Land's End, it has a wide distribution on maritime
lichens in the British Isles, although it has not been recorded from Wales
(Luxton 1990).
  Recorded from Scilly by Pugh and King (1988) on St Mary's and by Pugh
(1988) on St Mary's and Bryher, on supralittoral lichens.

[+]*Punctoribates* sp.
Many unidentified specimens from St Agnes - Samples 2, 4, 5, 6, 7, 8, 11, 12.
  Additionally, unidentified specimens probably of this family collected
on St Agnes from Samples 5, 6, 9.

Family Achipteriidae

Achipteria coleoptrata (Linnaeus, 1758)
Widely distributed in England, Scotland and Ireland and recorded from the Isles on Scilly by Luxton (1990) who collected specimens from dry moss at Hugh Town, St Mary's.

Achipteria nitens (Nicolet, 1855)
Widespread in England, but not recorded from Scotland or Ireland (Luxton 1990), and with one record from Wales (Luxton pers. comm.), this species has been recorded from the Isles of Scilly by Luxton (1990) who collected specimens on St Mary's from moss and thrift on The Garrison and from lichens on a lane wall.

Achipteria sp.
Many unidentified specimens collected on St Agnes from Samples 2, 4, 6, 7, 8, 9, 10, 12, 13.

+Family Galumnidae

+Acrogalumna longipluma (Berlese, 1904)
Recorded widely from England and from Co. Mayo in Ireland, but not recorded from Wales (Luxton pers. comm.).
    Now recorded on the Isles of Scilly from specimens collected on St Agnes from Samples 2, 4, 5, 6, 8, 10, 13.

Family Oribatellidae

Oribatella quadricornuta (Michael, 1880)
Widely distributed in England, Scotland and Ireland, but not recorded from Wales (Luxton 1990).
    First recorded from Scilly by Luxton (1990) who collected specimens on St Mary's from dry moss at Hugh Town. Now collected on St Agnes from Samples 2, 4, 5, 6, 7, 10, 13.

[+]Family Haplozetidae

[+]*?Xylobates* sp.
Unidentified specimens collected on St Agnes - Samples 3, 8, 9.

Family Oribatulidae

+Liebstadia similis (Michael, 1888)
'Among the commonest of oribatid mites in the British Isles' (Luxton 1989).
    Collected on St Agnes from Samples 2, 5, 7, 8.

[+]*Liebstadia* sp.
Unidentified specimens collected on St Agnes from Sample 2.

Oribatula saxicola Halbert, 1920
Widely distributed on maritime lichens in the British Isles (Luxton 1990).
    Recorded from the Isles of Scilly amongst supralittoral lichens on St Mary's (Pugh and King 1988, Pugh 1988).

Oribatula tibialis (Nicolet, 1855)
A widespread and common species in Britain (not recorded from Ireland) and recorded from the Isles of Scilly by Luxton (1990) who collected specimens from thrift on The Garrison, St Mary's.

Phauloppia lucorum (C.L.Koch, 1841)
A widespread and very common species in the British Isles (Luxton 1990). First recorded on Scilly by Pugh and King (1988) from St Mary's and by Pugh (1988) who collected specimens from supralittoral lichens on Bryher, Tresco, St Martin's, Great Arthur and St Mary's. Luxton (1990) collected material from moss, lichen, thrift and grass at 10 locations on St Mary's.

Phauloppia pilosa (C.L.Koch, 1841)
A species with limited southern distribution in Britain (Essex, Cornwall, Hampshire), Luxton (1990) recorded it on the Isles of Scilly from thin, dry moss at The Garrison, St Mary's.

Zygoribatula frisiae (Oudemans, 1900)
A normally non-maritime European species whose known distribution in the British Isles was previously limited to Bedfordshire and Norfolk (Luxton 1990). Recorded from supralittoral lichens on Scilly by Pugh and King (1988) (no precise locality) and by Pugh (1988) from Annet.

    Additionally, unidentified specimens of Oribatulidae from St Agnes - Samples 1, 3, 5, 8, 9, 10, 12.

Family Scheloribatidae

Scheloribates laevigatus (C.L.Koch, 1835)
Widespread and very common in the British Isles (Luxton 1990), this species was first recorded on the Isles of Scilly by Pugh and King (1988) who recorded specimens from supralittoral lichens on Tresco and by Pugh (1988) from Tresco, Bryher, Great Arthur and St Martin's. Luxton (1990) collected specimens from thrift on The Garrison, St Mary's.

Scheloribates pallidulus (C.L.Koch, 1841)
Of rather limited distribution in the British Isles and not recorded from Ireland,

this species has now been collected on the Isles of Scilly by Luxton (1990), who obtained specimens from lichens on rocks, Porthcressa Beach, St Mary's.

Scheloribates sp.
Unidentified specimens collected on St Agnes - Samples 8, 9, 10, 11.

Family Passalozetidae

Passalozetes bidactylus (de Coggi, 1900)
First authentically recorded in the British Isles by Luxton (1990) who collected specimens from dry tidal debris on Porthcressa Beach, St Mary's.

Family Scutoverticidae

Scutovertex sculptus Michael, 1879
Widespread and common in the British Isles and recorded from Scilly by Luxton (1990) who collected specimens on St Mary's from moss at Hugh Town and on The Garrison and from thrift, also on The Garrison.

Scutovertex sp.
Unidentified specimens collected on St Agnes from Samples 2, 8, 9, 12.

Family Phenopelopidae

Eupelops hirtus (Berlese, 1916)
The distribution of this species in the British Isles is limited to England and Wales where it is found widely (Luxton 1990). Recorded from Scilly by Luxton (1990) who collected specimens from bracken litter on The Garrison, St Mary's.

[+]*Eupelops* spp.
Unidentified specimens of probably two species collected on St Agnes from Samples 5, 6, 8.

Peloptulus phaeonotus (C.L.Koch, 1844)
A widespread, but not common species in the British Isles, it has now been recorded on the Isles of Scilly by Luxton (1990) who collected specimens on St Mary's from thin, dry moss on The Garrison and from grass in a rock crevice at Porthcressa Beach.

Peloptulus sp.
Unidentified specimens from St Agnes - Sample 5.
        Additionally, unidentified specimens of Phenopelopidae from St Agnes - Samples 5, 6, 7, 8, 9, 10, 12.

Order ASTIGMATA

Family Acaridae

+*Acarus farris* Oudemans, 1905
A cosmopolitan species found in a wide range of habitats including stored food products, compost, manure and leaf-litter.
    Adults and hypopial deutonymphs collected on St Agnes from Samples 1, 3, 4, 5, 7, 8.

[+]*Aleuroglyphus* sp.
St Agnes - Sample 3, a single specimen.

+*Rhizoglyphus robini* Claparède,1869
A widespread European species feeding mainly on fungi and rotting vegetation.
    Collected on St Agnes from Samples 3, 4.

Tyrophagus longior (Gervais, 1844)
A cosmopolitan species found frequently in stored food products and in haystacks, it was collected on Scilly by Pugh (1988) from amongst yellow lichens on Bryher and St Mary's.

Tyrophagus palmarum Oudemans, 1924
This cosmopolitan species is found largely in grassland, although it also occurs in stored grains and in haystacks. Pugh (1988) collected it on Scilly from tidal debris on Bryher.

Tyrophagus spp.
Unidentified specimens collected on St Agnes from most Samples - 3, 4, 5, 6, 8, 9, 11, 12.

Family Hyadesidae

Hyadesia tumida Benard, 1961
This European species was first recorded as British by Pugh (1988) who recorded it from Anglesey and also from Scilly where he collected it from littoral lichens on Annet.

Family Anoetidae

The Anoetidae are found generally in damp and wet habitats such as rotting wood, in *Drosophila* cultures, in rotting potatoes, etc. The phoretic deutonymphs are found on insects (Hyatt 1990a).

+*Histiostoma feroniarum* (Dufour, 1839)
A widely distributed European species now recorded from Scilly. Adult females collected on St Agnes from Samples 4, 8.

Rhopalanoetus lanceocrinus (Oudemans, 1914)
This European species was first recorded from the British Isles by Hyatt (1990a) who examined eight collections of deutonymphs from beetles, five being from St Agnes - four from *Geotrupes spiniger*, x.1962, and one from *Typhaeus typhoeus*, 18.xi.1962.

Also, unidentified anoetid deutonymphs have been removed from a specimen of *Geotrupes spiniger*, St Agnes, 1.xi.1963 (Hyatt 1990a).

Order PROSTIGMATA

With the exception of the Halacaridae, the majority of the Prostigmata are well known in the adult and nymphal stages as predators of a wide range of terrestrial microarthropods, whilst in some cases their larvae are parasitic on macroarthropods and vertebrates.

Family Scutacaridae

Pygmodispus calcaratus Paoli, 1911
Of the 16 species currently recognized in the genus *Pygmodispus*, seven are known from the Palaearctic region. Hyatt (1990a) recorded *P. calcaratus* in the British Isles from two specimens of *Geotrupes spiniger* collected on St Agnes, 15.x.1962 and 1.xi.1963.

Family Eupodidae

Eupodes variegatus (C.L.Koch, 1836)
A European species found in moss or under leaves and stones, recorded from Scilly by Pugh (1988) who collected what he believed to be this species on banks of tidal debris on St Martin's and on Great Arthur.

Eupodes sp.
Unidentified specimens collected on St Agnes from Samples 5, 6, 11.

[+]*Protereunetes* sp.
Unidentified specimens collected on St Agnes from Sample 5.
Also, unidentified eupodids from St Agnes - Sample 6.

Family Penthaleidae

Penthaleus sp.
Pugh (1988) collected a single specimen of this genus from tidal debris on

Tresco.

Family Bdellidae

Bdella decipiens Thorell, 1872
A northern European species known from Ireland and south-west England. Recorded from Scilly by Pugh and King (1988) from St Mary's, and by Pugh (1988) who collected specimens in the littoral zones on Tresco, Great Arthur and St Mary's.

Bdella interrupta Evans, 1952
A seashore species described from Wales. Recorded subsequently from Scilly by Pugh and King (1988) who examined specimens from St Mary's, and from Dorset, Devon, Cornwall and Scilly by Pugh (1988) who examined specimens from Tresco and St Mary's.

Neomolgus littoralis (Linnaeus, 1758)
The largest of the Bdellidae, this circumpolar species is found in Europe at least as far south as the English Channel: it had previously been recorded from Scotland and Devon and is now recorded from Scilly by Pugh and King (1988) who examined specimens from St Mary's, and from Dorset, Devon and Scilly by Pugh (1988) who collected specimens on St Martin's, St Mary's and Annet. The BM(NH) collections contain material from Cornwall, Devon, Kent (Dungeness), Essex (Mersea Id), Tyne and Wear (Whitburn), Cleveland (Teesmouth) and Highland (Rona).
    Also, unidentified bdellids from St Agnes - Samples 5, 6, 10, 12.

Family Rhagidiidae

Foveacheles (Mediostella) canestrini (Berlese & Trouessart, 1889)
A conspicuous and fast-moving species recorded from Scilly by Pugh (1988) who collected specimens in crevices in the upper littoral and in the supralittoral on St Mary's.

[+]*Rhagidia* sp.
Unidentified specimens collected on St Agnes - Sample 5.

+Family Labidostommidae

+*Labidostomma luteum* Kramer, 1879
A bright yellow, predatory inhabitant of moss, humus and soil, widely distributed in Europe, including the British Isles and the Channel Islands.
    Collected on St Agnes from Samples 11, 13.

[+]Family Cunaxidae

[+]*Cunaxoides* sp.
Unidentified specimens collected on St Agnes - Sample 6.

[+]Family Nanorchestidae

[+]*Nanorchestes* sp.
Unidentified specimens collected on St Agnes - Sample 9.

[+]Family Pachygathidae

[+]*Bimichaelia* sp.
Unidentified specimens collected on St Agnes - Samples 2, 5, 6.

[+]Family Stigmaeidae

[+]*Raphignathus* sp.
Unidentified specimens collected on St Agnes - Sample 5.
  Also unidentified stigmaeids from St Agnes - Sample 11.

Family Anystidae

Anystis sp.
Recorded from supralittoral lichens on the Isles of Scilly by Pugh and King (1988), but no further data given. This could refer to the specimens of *Erythracarus* (below) recorded by Pugh (1988).

Erythracarus sp.
Several specimens collected on Bryher by Pugh (1988) from lichens in the supralittoral zone.

Family Myobiidae

The Myobiidae are ectoparasites of mammals and seem to feed mainly on sebaceous secretions at the bases of hairs and seldom, if ever, suck blood.

Crocidurobia blairi (Radford, 1936)
Described from nymphs, males and females collected on a number of lesser white-toothed shrews *Crocidura suaveolens cassiteridum* on St Mary's in 1924 by W.N.Blair, the brother of Dr K.G.Blair, the entomologist, and brought to the attention of C.D.Radford by Harry Britten senior of Manchester Museum (Radford 1936). As far as can be determined, the only subsequent material of this species that has been collected is a series of about 17 males and 20 females

from the same host on St Mary's, made by Miss P.D.Jenkins (BM(NH) Mammal Section) on 1.x.1973.

Family Cheyletidae

+*Cheyletus trouessarti* Oudemans, 1902
Collected on St Agnes from Samples 7, 9.
  Unidentified cheyletids also collected on St Agnes - Sample 11.

Family Erythraeidae

Abrolophus harrisoni (Hull, 1918)
Described originally from saltmarshes on Tyneside, Pugh (1988) has assigned specimens collected in Cornwall and on St Mary's to this species, although its status is uncertain.

Abrolophus rubripes (Berlese & Trouessart, 1889)
Known previously from the coasts of France and in the British Isles from Ireland (Halbert 1915) and Devon (Evans and Browning 1954), this seashore species is now recorded from Cornwall and Scilly by Pugh (1988) who examined specimens from St Martin's and St Agnes.

+*Bochartia ?adrastus* Southcott, 1946
Specimens possibly referrable to this species collected on St Agnes - Sample 5.

[+]*Leptus* sp.
Adults collected on St Agnes from Samples 2, 4, 5. The adults and nymphs of this genus are predators on small arthropods, whilst the larvae parasitize larger arthropods, e.g. Lepidoptera and Diptera.

Family Trombidiidae

[+]*Camerotrombidium* sp.
Collected on St Agnes - Sample 4.

Trombidium kneissli (Krausse, 1915)
Non-maritime and described originally from Germany, Pugh and King (1988) tentatively identified this species from tidal debris, but gave no precise locality, whilst Pugh (1988) recorded a single specimen from the upper supralittoral among scattered and dry tidal debris on Tresco, although he queried his identification. These constitute the first, although unconfirmed, records from the British Isles.

Trombidium sp. *s.lat.*
Several specimens from St Agnes - Sample 4, and also from the underside of
a slab of granite on Wingletang Down.

Family Trombiculidae

+*Trombicula (Neotrombicula) autumnalis* (Shaw, 1790)
The common harvest mite. Widely distributed in the British Isles, parasitic in
the larval stage (including on humans) and predatory in nymphal and adult
stages.
    Collected on St Agnes - Sample 9.

Family Halacaridae

Copidognathus rhodostigma (Gosse, 1855)
A littoral crevice species known from the North Sea, the Atlantic coast of
France, from Plymouth (Fountain 1949; Marine Biological Association 1957),
and now recorded by Pugh (1988) from Cornwall and on Bryher in the Isles of
Scilly.

Halacarellus basteri basteri (Johnston, 1836)
The nominate form of this species is widely distributed on both sides of the
North Atlantic and in the Black Sea (Newell 1947). It is also known from Devon
(Colman 1940; Fountain 1949; Marine Biological Association 1957).
    First recorded from the Isles of Scilly by Brady (1875) and now collected
by Pugh (1988) on algae in the lower littoral zone on Bryher as well as in
Cornwall, Devon and Dorset.

Halacarus ctenopus Gosse, 1855
Recorded from the Isles of Scilly (Brady 1875) and from Plymouth (Fountain
1949; Marine Biological Association 1957).

Lohmanella falcata (Hodge, 1863)
A cosmopolitan species recorded from Antarctica, North America, the British
Isles, the Mediterranean and the Black Seas (Newell 1947).
    Recorded from Plymouth (Fountain 1949; Marine Biological Association
1957) and from Scilly by Brady (1875), whilst more recently Pugh (1988)
collected it in sublittoral sediments on St Martin's.

Rhombognathoides seahami (Hodge, 1860)
A common species, especially on littoral algae. Recorded from the Isles of
Scilly by Brady (1875) and recently from Cornwall, Devon and Dorset by Pugh
(1988).

SUMMARY

To date 169 species of mites are recorded from the Isles of Scilly, and of these 56 are recorded for the first time. Additionally, a further 42 taxa approximately are identified to genus or family level only.

	Previously recorded taxa		Newly recorded taxa			Total
	To species	To genus	To species	To genus	To family	
Mesostigmata	44	1	37	12	-	94
Metastigmata	6	-	-	-	-	6
Cryptostigmata	44	-	12	13	4	73
Astigmata	4	-	3	1	-	8
Prostigmata	15	3	4	8	-	30
Totals	113	4	56	34	4	211

Six species, all Mesostigmata, constitute new records for the British Isles.

ACKNOWLEDGEMENTS
I am grateful to Mr D.Macfarlane, C.A.B. International Institute of Entomology, for valuable assistance with the identification of the Prostigmata and Cryptostigmata, and to my former colleague Bernice Brewster for sorting and preparing much of the material. Special thanks go to Dr M. Luxton for his valuable comments on the manuscript and for allowing quotes from his unpublished notes on selected species of oribatids (Cryptostigmata), referred to herein as Luxton pers. comm. Finally, thanks also to Dr Frank A. Turk for reading the manuscript and suggesting some improvements which have been incorporated, and Mrs Stella M.Turk for introducing me to *Cornish Studies.*

REFERENCES

Bhattacharyya, S.K. 1963. A revision of the British mites of the genus *Pergamasus* Berlese *s.lat.* *Bulletin of the British Museum (Natural History)* Zoology 2: pp. 131-242.

Brady, G.S.1875. A review of the British marine mites with descriptions of some new species. *Proceedings of the Zoological Society of London* 1875: pp. 301-311.

Bregetova, N.G. *et al.* 1977. Gamasid mites (Gamasoidea). Precise determinations. *Opred. Faune SSSR* 61: pp. 1-247. [Russian].

Bristowe, W.S. 1929. The spiders of the Scilly Islands. *Proceedings of the Zoological Society of London* 1929: pp. 149-164.

Bristowe, W.S. 1935. Further notes on the spiders of the Scilly Islands. *Proceedings of the Zoological Society of London* 1935: pp. 219-232.

Browning, E. 1956. On a collection of Arachnida and Myriapoda from Jersey, Channel Islands, with a check list of the Araneae. *Bulletin Annuel de la Société Jersiaise* 16: pp. 377-394.

Colman, J. 1940. On the faunas inhabiting intertidal seaweeds. *Journal of the Marine Biological Association of the United Kingdom* 24: pp. 129-183.

Curry, J.P. 1976. The arthropod fauna of some common grass and weed species of pasture. *Proceedings of the Royal Irish Academy* 76B: pp. 1-35.

Evans, G.O. 1957. On the genus *Scarabaspis* Womersley (Acarina - Mesostigmata). *Annals and Magazine of Natural History* (12) 10: pp. 409-416.

Evans, G.O. 1958. A revision of the British Aceosejinae (Acarina: Mesostigmata). *Proceedings of the Zoological Society of London* 131: pp. 177-229.

Evans, G.O. and Browning, E. 1954. Some intertidal mites from south west England. *Bulletin of the British Museum (Natural History)* Zoology 1: pp. 413-422.

Evans, G.O. and Hyatt, K.H. 1956. British mites of the genus *Pachylaelaps* (Gamasina: Pachylaelaptidae). *Entomologist's Monthly Magazine* 92: pp. 118-129.

Evans, G.O. and Hyatt, K.H. 1960. A revision of the Platyseinae (Mesostigmata: Acesejinae) based on material in the collections of the British Museum (Natural History). *Bulletin of the British Museum (Natural History)* Zoology 6: pp. 25-101.

Evans, G.O. and Till, W.M. 1966. Studies on the British Dermanyssidae (Acari:Mesostigmata). Part II. Classification. *Bulletin of the British Museum (Natural History)* Zoology 14: pp. 107-370.

Evans, G.O. and Till, W.M. 1979. Mesostigmatic mites of Britain and Ireland (Chelicerata:Acari-Parasitiformes). An introduction to their external morphology and classification. *Transactions of the Zoological Society of London* 35: pp. 139-270.

Fountain, H.C. 1949. Notes on the Plymouth marine fauna. Halacaridae (Arachnida:Acarina). *Journal of the Marine Biological Association of the United Kingdom* 34: pp. 808-809.

Hull, J.E. 1918. Terrestrial Acari of the Tyne Province. *Transactions of the Natural History Society of Northumberland, Durham and Newcastle-upon-Tyne* 5, 1: pp. 13-88.

Halbert, J.N. 1915. Clare Island Survey, Part 39 ii Acarinida: Section II - Terrestrial and marine Acarina. *Proceedings of the Royal Irish Academy* 31: pp. 45-136.

Halbert, J.N. 1920. The Acarina of the seashore. *Proceedings of the Royal Irish Academy* 35, Sect. B: pp. 106-152.

Hirschmann, W. and Krauss, W. 1965. Bestimmungstafeln von 55 *Pachylaelaps*-Arten. *Acarologie* 7, Teil 8: pp. 1-5.

Hirschmann, W. and Zirngiebl-Nicol, I. 1969. Die Gattung *Uropoda* (Latreille, 1806). *Acarologie* 12: p. 24.

Hughes, A.M. 1976. The mites of stored food and houses. *Technical Bulletin, Ministry of Agriculture, Fisheries and Food* 9, p. 400.

Hyatt, K.H. 1956a. British mites of the genera *Halolaelaps* Berlese and Trouessart, and *Saprolaelaps* Leitner (Gamasina-Rhodacaridae). *Entomologist's Gazette* 7: pp. 7-26.

Hyatt, K.H. 1956b. British mites of the genus *Pachyseius* Berlese, 1910 (Gamasina-Neoparasitidae). *Annals and Magazine of Natural History.* (12) 9: pp. 1-6.

Hyatt, K.H. 1959. Mesostigmatid mites associated with *Geotrupes stercorarius* (L.) (Col. Scarabaeidae). *Entomologist's Monthly Magazine* 95: pp. 22-23.

Hyatt, K.H. 1980. Mites of the subfamily Parasitinae (Mesostigmata:Parasitidae) in the British Isles. *Bulletin of the British Museum (Natural History)* Zoology 38: pp. 237-378.

Hyatt, K.H. 1987. Mites of the genus *Holoparasitus* Oudemans, 1936 (Mesostigmata:Parasitidae) in the British Isles. *Bulletin of the British Museum (Natural History)* Zoology 52: pp. 139-164.

Hyatt, K.H. 1990a. Mites associated with terrestrial beetles in the British Isles. *Entomologist's Monthly Magazine* 126: pp. 133-147.

Hyatt, K.H. 1990b. Further observations on the terrestrial mite fauna of Headley Heath, Surrey. *The London Naturalist* 69: pp. 91-94.

Hyatt, K.H. 1990c. Additional records of British mites of the subfamily Parasitinae (Mesostigmata: Parasitidae). *Naturalist, Hull* 115: pp. 81-87.

Hyatt, K.H. and Emberson, R.M. 1988. A review of the Macrochelidae (Acari:Mesostigmata) of the British Isles. *Bulletin of the British Museum (Natural History)* Zoology 54: pp. 63-125.

Jones, P.E. (Ed.) 1980. *Provisional atlas of the Arachnida of the British Isles.* Part 1. *Pseudoscorpiones.* Institute of Terrestrial Ecology, Monks Wood.

Jones, R.E. and Pratley, P. 1987. Myriapods of the Isles of Scilly. *Bulletin of the British Myriapod Group* 4: pp. 7-15.

Karg, W. 1971. Acari (Acarina), Milben Unterordnung Anactinochaeta (Parasitiformes). Die freilebenden Gamasina (Gamasides), Raubmilben. *Tierwelt Deutschlands und der Angrenzenden Meeresteile* 59: pp. 1-475.

King, P.E. 1972. The marine flora and fauna of the Isles of Scilly - Pycnogonida. *Journal of Natural History* 6: pp. 621-624.

King, P.E., Fordy, M.R. and Morgan, C.I. 1981. The marine flora and fauna of the Isles of Scilly - Tardigrada. *Journal of Natural History* 15: pp. 145-150.

Lawrence, R.F. 1937. A new species of plume-footed mite from South Africa. *Annals of the South African Museum* 32: pp. 268-279.

Lousley, J.E. 1971. *Flora of the Isles of Scilly.* David and Charles, Newton Abbot.

Luxton, M. 1987. Oribatid mites from the Isle of Man. *Naturalist, Hull* 112: pp. 67-77.

Luxton, M. 1989. Oribatid mites (Acari:Cryptostigmata) from Orkney. *Naturalist, Hull* 114: pp. 85-91.

Luxton, M. 1990. Oribatid mites (Acari:Cryptostigmata) from the Isles of Scilly. *Naturalist, Hull* 115: pp. 7-11.

Macfadyen, A.M. 1952. The small arthropods of a *Molinia* fen at Cothill. *Journal of Animal Ecology* 21: pp. 87-117.

Marine Biological Association, U.K. 1957. Sub-phylum Arachnida. In: *Plymouth marine fauna,* 3rd ed.: pp. 262-263.

Martyn, K.P. 1988. *Provisional atlas of the ticks (Ixodoidea) of the British Isles.* Institute of Terrestrial Ecology, Monks Wood.

Newell, I.M. 1947. A systematic and ecological study of the Halacaridae of eastern North America. *Bulletin of the Bingham Oceanographic Collection,* Yale University 10: pp. 1-232.

Parry, B.W. 1979. A revision of the British species of the genus *Phthiracarus* Perty, 1841 (Cryptostigmata:Euptyctima). *Bulletin of the British Museum (Natural History)* Zoology 35: pp. 232-262.

Pickard-Cambridge, O. 1897. On a new genus and species of Acaridea. *Proceedings of the Zoological Society of London* 1897: pp. 939-941.

Pugh, P.J.A. 1988. The shore-dwelling Acari of the Isles of Scilly and the south-west peninsula. *Journal of Natural History* 22: pp. 931-948.

Pugh, P.J.A. and King, P.E. 1988. Acari of the British supralittoral. *Journal of Natural History* 22: pp. 107-122.

Radford, C.D. 1936. Notes on mites of the genus *Myobia.* Part IV. *North Western Naturalist,* 11: pp. 144-151.

Rood, J.P. and Burtt, E.T. 1965. Host relationships of *Ixodes arvicolae* Warburton on the Scilly Isles. *Parasitology, Cambridge* 55: pp. 595-599.

Smith, K.G.V. and Smith, V. 1983. *A bibliography of the entomology of the smaller British offshore islands.* Classey, Faringdon.

Thomas, C. 1985. *Exploration of a drowned landscape - Archaeology and history of the Isles of Scilly.* Batsford, London.

Till, W.M. 1988. Additions to the British and Irish mites of the genus *Veigaia* (Acari:Veigaiidae) with a key to species. *Acarologia* 29: pp. 3-12.

Turk, F.A. 1948. Two new species of ticks (Ixodidae). *Parasitology, Cambridge* 38: pp. 243-245.
Turk, F.A. 1953. A synonymic catalogue of British Acari.*Annals and Magazine of Natural History* (12) 6: pp. 1-26 and 81-99.